CHAUCER'S
House of Fame

CHAUCER'S
House of Fame
*The Poetics of
Skeptical Fideism*

Sheila Delany

*The University of Chicago Press
Chicago and London*

The University of Chicago Press, Chicago 60637
The University of Chicago Press, Ltd., London
© 1972 by The University of Chicago
All rights reserved. Published 1972
Printed in the United States of America

International Standard Book Number: 0–226–14181–0
Library of Congress Catalog Card Number: 72–84406

To Paul

Contents

Acknowledgments

I should like to acknowledge the help of Professors A. Kent Hieatt, now of the University of Western Ontario, and Howard Schless, of Columbia University, who read the dissertation from which this book evolved. The President's Research Grant Committee of Simon Fraser University kindly provided a grant for typing the manuscript. And to Charles Muscatine, who taught me how to read Chaucer, it is a real pleasure to express my gratitude.

I

Introduction

Since art holds a mirror up to critics as well as to life, it is hardly surprising that generations of readers have found their own images reflected in Chaucer's work. The history of Chaucer criticism forms a pattern of judgments that can be read feature by feature, as a medieval physiognomist would do, the shifting dialectic of esthetic taste reproducing in small the pattern of cultural change. Such variety of opinion Chaucer himself, always alert to the vicissitudes of fame, might have appreciated with appropriate irony. Yet although we may congratulate ourselves on seeing a more complete picture of Chaucer than our predecessors did, the very perception of dialectical tension in art, in criticism, or in history is as much a historically conditioned response as any earlier view of the poet. There is, therefore, some risk of partiality in suggesting that the tradition central to Chaucer's *House of Fame* is a critical and skeptical tradition, rooted in the awareness of coexistent contradictory truths and resulting in the suspension of final rational judgment. Nonetheless, to make this suggestion is not simply to impose a modern view on Chaucer's work, for the skeptical tradition is amply stated in the poet's own time: it is found in cosmology, metaphysics, encyclopedic compilations, poetry, and popular treatises. Like many of our own attitudes, that tradition was the product of historical and cultural events that had impaired certain established models of authority and trust. Far from being irrelevant, our own historical experience may be one of the most useful critical tools we possess.

Introduction

By Chaucer's "skepticism" I do not mean agnosticism or overt heresy at one extreme (for Chaucer displayed neither); or, at the other extreme, a vague tendency to quibble or scoff at received truths. I mean, rather, that sense of the unreliability of traditional information which Chaucer deliberately incorporates into the style and structure of his poetry.[1] It is no longer necessary to justify the view of Chaucer as a poet conscious of his artistic role and power. That has been done in the work of Charles Muscatine, E. Talbot Donaldson, D. W. Robertson, and other contemporary critics. Most critics, however, view the *House of Fame* as a peculiarly puzzling or untypical work, not really amenable to the critical methods so fruitfully applied elsewhere; Muscatine speaks for many when he remarks of the *House of Fame* that "incoherency is the central fact of its character."[2] What may require justification, therefore, is an interpretation of the *House of Fame* as a work which reveals Chaucer's artistic consciousness, for to many readers the poem seems confused stylistically, struc-

1. This definition will distinguish my approach from that of Mary E. Thomas, *Medieval Skepticism and Chaucer* (New York, 1950), who accepts "perplexity, criticism, agnosticism and disbelief" as forms of skepticism, and who makes no attempt to relate a more rigorous definition of skepticism to Chaucer's poetics.
2. Charles Muscatine, *Chaucer and the French Tradition* (Berkeley, 1958), p. 114. Other opinions are that the poem is "Chaucer's most curious and elusive poem" and that it has an "amorphous structure" (Donaldson, *Chaucer's Poetry* [New York, 1958], 953-55); that it is "nearly a major disaster" (Raymond Preston, *Chaucer* [London, 1952], p. 39). On the other hand, several recent studies of the poem have tried to show its unity of theme and structure, among them Paul G. Ruggiers, "The Unity of Chaucer's *House of Fame*," SP, 50 (1953): 16-29; B. G. Koonce, *Chaucer and the Tradition of Fame* (Princeton, 1966); and Lawrence K. Shook, "The House of Fame," in *A Companion to Chaucer Studies*, ed. Beryl Rowland (New York, 1958). While I fully agree with the premise of these writers that the *House of Fame* has a theme and that it has what Suzanne Langer calls "significant form," I do not think that its theme and form can be adequately defined as a single topic, such as fame, glory, love, wisdom, or even the art of writing poetry. Theme and form are rather to be apprehended in the structure of each part of the narrative in which these and other subjects are taken up. In that repeated structural pattern is the meaning of the poem.

turally, and thematically. It is a dream-vision, but it opens with an ironically disrespectful résumé of medieval dream-lore. The subject of fame is not treated in depth until the third and last section of the poem. The Narrator's allegorical journey to Fame's palace would seem logically to belong at the start of the poem, but begins one-third of the way through it. The Narrator's experience in the Temple of Venus, which occupies Book I, seems to have no dramatic function in the poem, nor does the Eagle's humorous lecture in Book II; and the poem itself is unfinished.

My approach to these and other problems in the poem is based on a definition of fame which includes both rumor and reputation, but which extends beyond these notions. Fame, I suggest, is to be understood as the body of traditional knowledge that confronted the educated fourteenth-century reader. The idea of fame as tradition at large occurs in several classical loci, all of them well known to the medieval reader in the works of curriculum authors.[3] It is further illustrated in the *Polychronicon*, a widely read history of the world compiled near the middle of the fourteenth century by the English monk Ralph Higden, and translated into English in 1387 by John Trevisa.[4] Discussing the question of whether Paradise existed on earth, Higden cites several kinds of "witness" (evidence), among them the survival of the tradition itself:

> The fourthe witnesse and preef, that suche a place is in erthe that is y-cleped Paradys, is olde fame and longe durynge ["fama diuturna"]; for me schal trowe olde fame, that is nought withseide; but fame of Paradys hath i-dured withoute withseienge sexe thousand yere and more; for from the bygynnynge of the world anon to oure dayes it hath endured. And fame that is false dureth nought so longe, for it

3. See, for example, Virgil, *Aeneid* 6. 14: "Daedalus, ut fama est, fugiens"; Horace, *Satires* 2. 1. 36: "pulsis (vetus est ut fama) Sabellis"; Livy, *History* 1. 1. 6: "Duplex inde fama est."
4. The Latin text, together with Trevisa's translation, is edited in the Rolls Series, vol. 41, nos. 1–9.

fallith out of mynde, other is despreved by sothe-
nesse i-knowe.

Bk. 1, chap. 10

In asserting this proof of the existence of Paradise, Higden
displays a cheerful faith in fame and in human nature:
what survives must be true, for what is false will inevitably
fail to survive. Even for Higden, though, such confidence
is too simple always to account for discrepancy or improbability in historical sources, of which "more certeyn som is
i-holde than othir." In setting forth guidelines for choice,
Higden recommends that we believe whatever does not
contradict known fact or Christian doctrine; but, he notes,
divergency is not necessarily to be condemned, for there
may be logical reasons for error. Thus Higden walks a
tightrope with considerable grace, preserving a delicate
balance between critical evaluation and the will to believe.
As for his own role, Higden remains uncommitted. His
purpose is not to ascertain the truth, but to collect what
others have written:

> Wherfore in the writynge of this storie I take
> nought uppon me to aferme for sooth all that I
> write, but such as I have seie and i-rad in dyverse
> bookes, I gadere and write with oute envie, and
> comoun to othere men. For the apostel seith
> nought, "All that is write to oure lore is sooth," but
> he seith "Al that is i-write to oure lore it is i-write."

This flexibility is made possible by Higden's notion of the
historian's purpose, which is less to ascertain what really
happened than to present a pageant of worthy sayings and
deeds for the benefit of posterity; for

> in oure tyme, art, sciense and lawe were i-falle,
> ensample of noble dedes were nought i-knowe;
> nobilite and faire manere of spekynge were all
> i-lost; but the mercy of God had i-ordyned us of
> lettres in remedie of unparfightnesse of mankynde.

4

Although such praise of books is a commonplace in medieval literature, it is not simply rhetoric here, for it suggests the mythographic function of much medieval historiography. To Higden, as to any mythographer, differences in external detail are of little importance in comparison with the moral structure of events.

Many late medieval writers, however—aware, like Higden, that tradition may be fallible—could not so casually accept fame as evidence, or evidence as proof; nor could they remain so calmly impartial. The poet's task, unlike the historian's, is not merely to collect opinions, but to choose among them in order to construct his own vision of the truth. If wide reading among historical and literary sources provided the medieval poet with a wealth of material, it must also have indicated the equivocal nature of tradition, or fame. It is the purpose of the *House of Fame*, I would suggest, to explore some traditions in which Chaucer was to work as scholar and poet. Further, the poem attempts to establish for the artist a rhetorical and intellectual stance that can accommodate both traditional material and a skeptical approach to that material. From this point of view many of its stylistic and structural features are neither inappropriate nor inconsistent. They are instead part of a coherent effort to portray a subject whose salient trait is ambiguity. Like Matthew Arnold five centuries later, Chaucer in his attitude toward tradition seems to occupy a position "between two worlds, one dead/The other powerless to be born." We have no direct autobiographical statement that Chaucer felt such a predicament, nor is it the kind of feeling that could as yet be clearly expressed in poetry. Since the economic, intellectual, and political institutions of the High Middle Ages had been only partly destroyed and partly replaced,[5] the poet did not have to invent new myths. He did have to assign priorities among

5. Studies that help to define the radical social and cultural changes that occurred during the thirteenth and fourteenth centuries are Maurice Dobb, *Studies in the Development of Capitalism* (New York, 1947), chap. 1-3 and passim; Walter Ullman, *A History of Political*

existing traditions and to adjust them to new necessities. That task, recorded in the body of Chaucer's work, is announced in the *House of Fame.*

But to assign priorities among existing traditions was not a task limited to poets. It was the major effort of certain late medieval philosophers as well, and it is in their work that the nature of medieval skeptical fideism is most lucidly defined. In philosophy as well as in literary study, scholars were able to observe that some traditions are not susceptible of proof and that some traditions are flatly contradicted by others. Their task, like Chaucer's, was to establish a balanced intellectual position, one that could accommodate traditional belief and the skeptical attitude toward belief that was the inevitable result of their logical investigations. Their solution, like Chaucer's, was skeptical fideism. A brief survey of the motives and methods of these philosophers will help to clarify the problem; for the philosophers state their dilemma openly, while Chaucer's statement is made only through symbolic action. We may begin, then, with the structure of logical argument, in order to define alternatives which Chaucer will present in the structure of his poetry.

Thought: the Middle Ages (London, 1965); A. C. Crombie, *Medieval and Early Modern Science* (Cambridge, Mass., 1953) 2 vols; Etienne Gilson, *History of Christian Philosophy in the Middle Ages* (London, 1955); Frederick Antal, *Florentine Painting and Its Social Background* (London, 1948); Carl Stephenson, *Borough and Town, A Study of Urban Origins* (Cambridge, Mass., 1933).

2

Skeptical Fideism in the Middle Ages

The medieval skeptical tradition is not a continuation of the teachings of Greek skeptical philosophers. In that formal sense, the tradition of skepticism was practically unknown during the Middle Ages, though traces of it have been found.[1] Yet without knowing the specific arguments of the classical school, medieval skepticism does, like its predecessor, insist on the limits and contingency of human knowledge, whether the source of that knowledge be experience, natural reason, or traditional authority. The central difference between classical and late medieval skepticism is that the Christian concept of divine omnipotence permitted the medieval philosopher to go beyond purely logical concepts. He did not need to limit himself to an agnostic assertion of contingency, but could move to a fideistic statement of the mutually exclusive claims of logic and faith, conceding the latter to be superior. Despite a potentially revolutionary premise, then, the medieval skeptical philosopher generally stopped short of a revolutionary conclusion. He was able, through the separation of truths, to subordinate revolutionary logic to conservative doctrine.

Although medieval skepticism cannot convincingly be traced to the ancient Academy, its methodology can be

1. There is some evidence that a manuscript of the skeptical philosopher Sextus Empiricus was known; see Charles Jourdain, "Sextus Empiricus et la Philosophie Scholastique," in *Excursions . . . à travers le Moyen Age* (Paris, 1888). And Etienne Gilson, *History*, p. 447, points out that some arguments of the ancient skeptics were transmitted to the Middle Ages by their great opponent Augustine.

found there in the discipline of dialectics, which was transmitted to the Middle Ages primarily in the work of Aristotle and his commentators. The importance of dialectics is not simply that its aim (as defined by Plato and Aristotle) is to force, by questioning and scientific scrutiny, the reevaluation or refinement of received ideas. It is that Christian metaphysics, founded on myth rather than on logical principles, cannot absorb rational investigation beyond a certain point. In order to survive, it must sooner or later reject such investigation, and in the confrontation of Christian doctrine and classical logic we may locate the origin of medieval skepticism as a conscious, developed philosophical position. That confrontation was not acute until the late twelfth and thirteenth centuries, but even from the earliest times the potential dangers of dialectical method had been evident to Christian doctors. It could be used (abused, they would say) to contradict such doctrinal teachings as were not logically demonstrable. Some early Christian apologists (for example, Tatian and Tertullian) considered dialectics the parent of heresy; and though Augustine accepted dialectics as a valuable tool against heretics, even he stated that while "it is easy to learn the nature of valid inference even in schools which are outside of the Church . . . the truth of propositions is a matter to be discovered in the sacred books of the Church."[2] To deprive dialectics of the power to distinguish between true and false propositions amounts to denying its very reason for existence.

The point is elaborated by John Scotus Erigena (810–877), who warns that dialectics, like other gifts of God, can be used for good or for ill.

> A person skilled in the art of disputation (which is called dialectics) can use it well if he wishes (for it was given man to that end by God) when he educates the ignorant with it, and when he distin-

---

2. *On Christian Doctrine*, trans. D. W. Robertson, Jr. (New York, 1958), Book 2, chapter 31. Unless otherwise noted, all translations in the text are my own.

guishes true from false, analyzes what is confused, connects what is separated, and seeks the truth in all things. But he may, on the other hand, use it wickedly (though it was not given for that) when, showing false things to be true, he sends people into error, confusing and beclouding their senses with false reasoning, so that their inner eye (that is, the soul) cannot grasp the notion of pure truth.[3]

Erigena's fears had already been justified by the monk Gottschalk, whose heretical treatise on predestination Erigena had refuted with the tract just quoted. A later fulfillment of Erigena's warning was the attempt by Berengar of Tours (1000–1088) to apply dialectical reasoning to the mystery of the Eucharist. The orthodox explanation of the mystery is that the accidents of bread (its physical properties) remain, but that its substance (its real being) changes from that of bread to that of Christ's body. To believe that the properties of bread inhere in the substance of Christ's body is precisely the test of faith and constitutes the miracle, for according to logic, accidents cannot exist apart from a corresponding substance. A second substance may be added to the first, but the original substance cannot be removed. Berengar's solution was to deny the real physical presence of Christ's body in the bread, claiming that it was present only symbolically. In the ensuing controversy, volumes of protest and refutation were launched against Berengar. His opponents—no less dialecticians than himself—accused him, among other things, of intellectual pride and the abuse of reason: "By seeking refuge in dialectics," wrote the Italian ecclesiastic and scholar Lanfranc, "you have abandoned the holy writers." After being condemned, Berengar made several retractions and a formal profession of faith.

A similar controversy developed over the theory of Roscelin (1050–1120), a teacher of Abelard, who demonstrated by logic that since three essences cannot inhere in a single

---

3. Erigena, *Liber de Praedestinatione*, PL 122: 382.

form, then the Holy Trinity must be considered a triple form. The obvious interpretation of this theory is that Roscelin taught tritheism, though he denied this at the Council of Soissons and escaped condemnation.

The dialectician whose name is most widely known today is Peter Abelard (1079–1142), and he is probably better known as the lover of Héloïse than as a brilliant dialectician. Abelard was neither a skeptic nor a fideist, for he firmly believed that the lessons of Christian doctrine could be confirmed by reason. Nor did Abelard know many of the major Aristotelian works, for these had not been translated before his death. He was nonetheless an Aristotelian, and though his knowledge was confined mainly to the "logica vetus," his approach to Christian doctrine was sufficiently rationalistic to offend ecclesiastical authorities. Abelard's treatment of traditional materials in the *Sic et Non* (1122) illustrates the frame of mind that was so threatening to the orthodox. *Sic et Non* is a collection of contradictory statements on various subjects ranging from the relation of faith and reason to whether Joseph and Mary had intercourse. The texts, drawn mostly from the Church fathers, are not reconciled with one another but are simply juxtaposed, mosaic-fashion. The purpose of the collection—not the first of its kind—was to evolve a critical method that could account for inconsistency among doctrinal authorities. In the Prologue to his work Abelard sets forth certain principles by which these discordant texts are to be studied.[4] The reader, he says, must bear in mind the possibility of scribal error, of figurative language, of the author's reliance on erroneous received opinion, of his ignorance of early periods and foreign customs. If the techniques of textual and historical criticism fail to produce a satisfactory adjustment between conflicting texts, then the more convincing text must be chosen. Here Abelard's rationalism reaches its limit, for he

---

4. *Petri Abelardi Sic et Non*, ed. E. Henke and G. Lindenkohl (Marburg, 1851).

does not suggest that both authorities may be wrong. One or another must be believed on the basis of what is, finally, a subjective judgment:

> Through the above methods the diligent reader will attempt to resolve the controversies in the writings of the Fathers. If the controversy should be so blatant that it cannot be solved by reason, then the authorities are to be compared, and the one which offers better proof and greater assurance is to be believed.

Abelard defends himself against the anticipated charge of rashness in displaying these statements which "not only seem different from one another but indeed are opposed to one another." He justifies his effort by observing that doubt is the first key to wisdom, for

> by doubting we arrive at questions; by questioning we grasp the truth: concerning which, Truth itself has said, 'Seek and you shall find, knock and it shall be opened to you.'

In another work (*Dialectica*, bk. 4), Abelard gives a moving defense of the role of dialectics, arguing that since reason is a divine gift, there can be no sin in knowing, only in doing; he adds, following Augustine, that dialectics offers faith a powerful weapon in the struggle against heresy.[5] But even though Abelard's intention in his work was surely orthodox, it was his willingness to rely on reason before faith that brought down on him the wrath of the Church. Particularly offensive to such a man as St. Bernard of Clairvaux must have been the knowledge that for Abelard there was no mystery that could not be elucidated by logic: "Nil videt per speculum, nil in aenigmate." If reason can support faith, as Abelard held, it can do so only within strict limits. Abelard agrees to find faith through reason, while the orthodox believer agrees to find reasons for his faith: "fides quarens intellectum." For the orthodox, faith

---

5. *Petrus Abelardus, Dialectica,* ed. L. M. de Rijk (Assen, 1956).

may be supported by logic but it cannot be simply the result of logic; for logic can work for or against faith, and in that respect it is an unreliable basis for faith. Abelard's opponents saw quite clearly—more clearly than Abelard himself —that the pursuit of dialectics must sooner or later require a radically new approach to faith: one that would deprive it of the support of reason by demonstrating that the two are finally incompatible. (That Abelard's enemies were correct is shown by the subsequent development of late medieval philosophy.) Thus if the rationalism of skeptical inquiry is not to end in agnosticism, it must end, paradoxically, in an antirational fideism. It is the inherent deprecation of reason in fideism that accounts for its having never enjoyed official sanction from the Church, despite the orthodoxy of its conclusions. As the *New Catholic Encyclopedia* (1967) notes, "Fideism goes too far in its negative attitude toward the credibility of faith." Epistemologically subordinate to faith, then, reason must serve or reinforce the higher power: philosophy must be, in the often-quoted phrase, "the handmaid of theology."

From the beginning of the Christian era there had been well-founded reservations about the role of dialectics. Although the dangers of the method remained latent for the most part, such notable exceptions as the cases just mentioned ensured, from the eleventh century on, a steady stream of ecclesiastical literature which explored the subversive possibilities of dialectics, warned against its abuse, and accused one or another scholar of excessive reliance on human reason. During the late twelfth and thirteenth centuries, however, what had been rare became frequent, and the tendency of dialectical method became all too obvious. The catalyst was the translation from Greek and Arabic of the majority of Aristotle's most important works, together with commentaries upon those works and original treatises influenced by them. This body of material (a heterogeneous blend of Aristotelian, neo-Platonic, Arabic, and Hebrew thought) infused new energy into European intellectual life. It brought a materialist physics, psychology, economics, and political theory to the attention of medieval scholars; it gave them new opportunities to practice their skills, new alternatives to elaborate or refute. The Aristotelian corpus was also an open invitation to exercise dialectical method on forbidden subjects, for it provided a cosmology whose contradiction of Christian theory required some mediation between the two. Nothing short of outright rejection could be completely acceptable to the ecclesiastical hierarchy, whose first response was to prohibit the teaching of the new material in the universities. But no such prohibition could be fully effective, and other responses were soon found. One could (like William of Auvergne, Albert the Great, or Thomas Aquinas) refute philosophical conclusions with philosophical arguments, constructing an eclectic synthesis of Plato, Aristotle, and Christian doctrine. Or one could divide logic from doctrine, rejecting neither but allowing both to stand as different orders of truth.

This last approach, on which I want to focus, has come to be known as "the standard of double truth," a distortion that seems to have been imposed on such philosophers as Siger of Brabant and Boetius of Dacia by their ecclesiastical opponents. According to Bishop Tempier's preface to the list of propositions he condemned at Paris in 1277,

> They claim something to be known and true according to Aristotle, but not according to the Catholic faith, as if there were two contrary truths, and as if there were any truth in the texts of damnable pagans against the truth of Holy Writ.[6]

It seems clear, though, that no philosopher actually claimed that there could be two separate and equally valid

6. Latin text in H. Denifle, *Chartularium Universitatis Parisiensis*, 1: 543. The entire document is translated in *Medieval Political Philosophy: A Sourcebook* (New York, 1963), ed. Ralph Lerner and Muhsin Mahdi; the translation in my text is my own. On condemnations of the new learning, see E. Gilson, *History*, parts 6 and 9. On the standard of "double truth," see F. van Steenberghen, *Les Oeuvres et la Doctrine de Siger de Brabant* (Brussels, 1938) and *Siger de Brabant d'Après ses Oeuvres Inédites* (Louvain, 1942).

truths. It was asserted only that the truths of philosophy are necessary and evident, since they follow inevitably from the existing natural order; while the truth of doctrine, transcending both natural and logical orders, is absolute and superior to any other. Thus the truth of doctrine cannot be challenged by natural reason, nor need reason hesitate to pursue its arguments to their furthest conclusions. In this sense dialectics was freed of earlier restraints, a development which the *New Catholic Encyclopedia* interprets as follows: "By 1300 dialectics in the Middle Ages had lost its Biblical, patristic and humanistic moorings."

The intellectual acrobatics by which the freedom of dialectics was won are illustrated by a number of thirteenth- and fourteenth-century scholars, and nowhere more succinctly than in the work of Boetius of Dacia (thirteenth century; dates unknown). In his *Tractatus de Aeternitate Mundi*, the Swedish-born scholar treats a question which was central to the confrontation of Christianity and Aristotelianism; for the philosopher's opinion that the world is eternal directly opposes the Christian myth of creation ex nihilo. Boetius begins by defining the Scylla and Charybdis between which the Christian logician must navigate:

> It would be foolish to seek reasons for believing what ought to be believed from law [i.e., doctrine], for such things have no reason to them, and whoever does it seeks what is impossible to find. But it would be heretical to refuse to believe such things on the grounds that they are without reason.[7]

Hoping to avoid both foolishness and heresy, Boetius writes that he will neither seek demonstration where that is impossible, nor refuse to believe what is prescribed by faith. How will this be possible? "Faith is supported by miracles and not by reasons; what is held as a rational con-

7. All citations are translated from *Boetii de Dacia Tractatus de Aeternitate Mundi*, ed. Geza Sajo (Berlin, 1964).

clusion is not faith but knowledge." Since the two faculties operate at different epistemological levels, there can be no contradiction between them. They describe entirely different kinds of causality.

> Natural reason, considering only the power of natural causes, says that the world and first motion could not have been created new from those causes; Christian faith, considering a cause superior to nature, says that the world could have been made new from that cause; and they are not contradictory. And so two things are obvious: one, that natural philosophy does not contradict Christian faith about the eternity of the world; the other, that by natural reason it cannot be shown that the world and first motion were created new.

Later on in his argument, Boetius suggests another reason why faith must be preserved intact: the alternative is agnosticism.

> There are many things posited by faith which cannot be investigated by human reason; but where reason fails, faith fills in, which ought to demonstrate the superiority of divine power to human cognition. Nor because of this ought one to disbelieve the articles of faith (which are indemonstrable), because if one does so he will retain no law at all, for there is no law whose every article is demonstrable.

Boetius can therefore conclude with the philosophers, and according to reason, that the world is eternal; simultaneously he can affirm that, according to faith, it is not.

> We say, therefore, that the world is not eternal but created anew, even though this cannot be demonstrated by reasons, as was seen above, like other things that pertain to faith; indeed if they were demonstrable it would be not faith but knowledge. So that for faith neither logic nor dialectics nor demonstrations ought to be adduced, for these cre-

ate only opinion, and faith ought to be firmer than opinion. Otherwise faith would be nothing more than what is demonstrable.

What Boetius proposes, then, is a kind of peaceful co-existence:

> Therefore let the intelligent Christian not think of using his law to destroy the principles of philosophy, but let him save both faith and philosophy by attacking neither.

Boetius' colleague Siger de Brabant (c. 1240–c. 1282) also wrote a short treatise on the eternity of the world. In his other works Siger, like Boetius, recoils from the agnosticism that absolute skepticism brings. He concedes that no one can sincerely hold at the same moment two contradictory opinions; but faith is not opinion. Thus human reason sometimes leads to conclusions which must be denied ("ratio humana ducit in hoc quod debet negari")[8] and that which is marvelous or miraculous is not always impossible. In his treatise *De Aeternitate Mundi* Siger does not set out the conflict of faith and logic as clearly as Boetius does, but his minimal nod in the direction of orthodoxy plainly proceeds from principles similar to those of the Swedish scholar. Trying to prove that the human species must have been caused in a natural way, Siger remarks, "We say these things as the opinion of the Philosopher, although not asserting them as true."[9] Elsewhere Siger writes that

> nobody should attempt to investigate by reason what is above reason, nor to refute reasons to the contrary. But since a philosopher, however great he is, may always err in many matters, no one should deny the Catholic truth on account of some philo-

8. From Siger's *Questions* on Aristotle's *Metaphysics*, 3: 19. Quoted in F. van Steenberghen, *Siger de Brabant d'Après ses Oeuvres Inédites* (Louvain, 1942), vol. 1.
9. In C. Vollert, L. Kendzierski, and P. M. Byrne, eds. and trans., *St. Thomas Aquinas, Siger of Brabant, St. Bonaventure: On the Eternity of the World* (Milwaukee, 1964).

sophical reason, even though he does not see how to refute it.[10]

How little satisfactory such a rapprochement was to the Church, was shown when the work of both Siger and Boetius was condemned in 1277 and the two scholars were forced to flee for safety to Italy.

Like Bishop Tempier, the modern reader may wish to question the sincerity of such professions of faith as that of Boetius of Dacia. Prudence was, no doubt, a relevant consideration to him and to other scholars. Yet the distinction between natural probability and doctrinal certainty, on which so much depends, was dictated by more than the possibility of persecution. One cannot, in the last analysis, dispense with that distinction without having virtually dispensed with the traditional concept of God, for the notion of an omnipotent God carries with it, as corollary, a condition of universal contingency. If God is free to will or to do anything, then anything can change whenever God chooses to exercise his liberty. No creature, no idea is immune from that possibility. Convinced of God's omnipotence, the medieval logician could therefore hope to ascertain only probability. Today we have substituted the laws of matter for God's will, so that we are able to accept as virtually certain what the late medieval scholar could consider as only probable. Matter is, for us, far more predictable than God could be for many philosophers.

Although it was rejected by the ecclesiastical establishment in the great condemnation of Paris, the separation of truths remained clearly the readiest way for scholars to steer their course "between foolishness and heresy." As such it was used by John of Jandun (d. 1328), master at the University of Paris, admirer of Averroes, and associate of the famed political theorist Marsilius of Padua. Taking up the perennially important issue of whether the world was created from nothing, John writes,

10. From Cornelio A. Graiff, ed. *Siger de Brabant, Questions sur la Métaphysique* (Louvain, 1948), p. 140; cited also in Gilson, *History*, p. 720.

> The world is produced anew . . . by creation, which is equivocal generation and simple emanation. And this is not known by those who receive their faith about everything on the basis of sensible things. Whence it cannot be demonstrated, because it is above nature, and is faith and truth, and we ought to believe firmly that God has created everything from nothing, assenting to the saintly teachers of the faith.[11]

The distinction between doctrinal truth and logical necessity appears throughout John's work. A question which had long concerned scholars, because of its application to the theory of the Eucharist, was that of the independent existence of substance and accidents. This problem, John claims, is not resolvable by logic:

> This is not a philosophical principle, whereby accidents remain in the sacrament of the altar . . . this is not a matter of the senses and cannot be proved from sensible things. We must firmly believe this, without proof, assenting reverently to the teachers of the Holy Church. We gain merit from that which we believe and cannot demonstrate. There is no natural principle by which they resolve the matter, but only a supernatural and miraculous one. Aristotle and the Commentator, speaking naturally, did not see this, since they had to see philosophically, by means of sensible things.[12]

Again, treating the question whether the first principle is (like Aristotle's first mover) as limited and comprehensible as any other natural force, or whether (like the Christian God) it is of infinite power, John says,

> According to faith and truth I say that the first principle that is God . . . is of infinite power *simpliciter*. I cannot establish this by any proof, be-

11. *Questions on De Caelo*, 1: 29, in Stuart MacClintock, *Perversity and Error, Studies on the "Averroist" John of Jandun* (Bloomington, 1950), p. 89.
12. Ibid., p. 90 (from *Questions on Metaphysics*, 7: 1).

cause I do not know how, nor do I think that it is possible according to natural principles—but by faith alone do I thus assert and maintain it *simpliciter.*[13]

The English logician William of Ockham (1290–1350), whose logic and natural philosophy were to have a profound impact on European intellectual life, was always careful to mark the boundary between logic and doctrine. In the Prologue to his *Exposition* of Aristotle's *Physics*, Ockham distinguishes his personal beliefs from the strictly philosophical analysis to follow.

> No one may attribute to me the opinions that I am about to present, since I do not intend to express what I myself hold in accord with the Catholic faith, but only what I think the Philosopher has approved, or ought to have approved in accordance with his own principles.[14]

In another tract, to the question "Can it be proved by natural reason that there is only one God?" Ockham answers that the existence of God can indeed be proved logically (depending on one's definition of God), but it cannot be proved that there is only one God:

> We could go on *ad infinitum*, if there were not some one among beings to which nothing is prior or superior in perfection. But from this is does not follow that there is only one such being. This we hold only by faith.[15]

Or again, discussing whether intuitive cognition can be had of an object that does not exist, Ockham writes,

> In this question I assert two conclusions. The first is that there can be by the power of God intuitive knowledge concerning a nonexistent object; this I

13. Ibid., p. 92 (from *Questions on Physics*, 8: 22).
14. *Ockham, Philosophical Writings*, trans. Philotheus Boehner (London, 1957), p. 13.
15. Ibid., p. 126.

prove first by an article of faith: I believe in God, father almighty. . . .
The second conclusion is that intuitive knowledge cannot be caused or conserved naturally when the object is not existent.[16]

Later in the century Jean Buridan, the Parisian scientist and follower of Ockham in logic, answers in two different conclusions the question whether it is possible for something to be made from nothing.

The first conclusion is that it is possible for something to be made without a prior subject from which or in which it is made. And this conclusion I believe through faith and not through any proof except the authority of Holy Writ and of the doctors of the Catholic faith. Thus did God make and create the angels, the heaven and the world . . . . The second conclusion is that every thing that is made in nature must be made from a prior subject or in a prior subject.[17]

Buridan's pupil, the accomplished scholar, administrator and ecclesiastic Nicole Oresme, is equally reluctant to reject Christian teaching, though his scientific reasoning leads him to the brink of it. In his commentary on Aristotle's *De Caelo et Mundo*, Oresme shows that the theory of a stationary earth at the center of a rotating universe is indemonstrable, while the reverse hypothesis—that the planets move around the sun—is both possible and likely. At the end of his lengthy demonstration, though, Oresme hastily adds,

nevertheless everyone holds and I agree that it [the heaven] is moved and not the earth: *Deus enim firmavit orbem terre, qui non commovetur,* despite

16. The passage is from Ockham's Quodlibet 6, question 6, in *Selections from Medieval Philosophers*, ed. Richard McKeon (New York, 1930), p. 373.

17. Jean Buridan, *Physics* 1: 15, in Anneliese Maier, *Metaphysische Hintergründe der Spätscholastischen Naturphilosophie* (Rome, 1955), p. 16.

all reasonings to the contrary, for they are not evident proofs.[18]

For Oresme, as for most of his contemporaries, the supreme
authority is not natural reason but Genesis.

With the separation of truths as their declaration of
independence, progressive scholars of the thirteenth and
fourteenth centuries were able to pursue their arguments
as far as logically possible. Skeptical fideism offered a way
of saving both faith and reason, for while faith was no
longer to be supported by reason, neither was it to be denied
out of hand. As a separate mode of perception it could
remain valid on its own terms, neither requiring proof nor
infringing on it. The freedom thus achieved was, as we
have seen, a limited freedom insofar as rational argument
could not yet be accepted as final. Indeed logic was still
restrained by the very device that freed it, for as long as
doctrine was acknowledged to be supreme, and God's will
the highest cause, then reason and experience could attain
only relative validity. The thoroughgoing materialism required for the genuinely free exercise of logic would necessarily be reserved to later centuries; it would be developed
most fully in the work of Karl Marx and Friedrich Engels. ·
It is not by William of Ockham, therefore, that the principle of "Ockham's razor" has been most rigorously applied: *Pluralitas numquam ponenda sine necessitate.*

18. *Maistre Nicole Oresme, Le Livre du Ciel et du Monde,* ed. Albert
D. Menut and Alexander Denomy (Toronto, 1943), sec. 144B.

3

The Poetics of Skeptical Fideism

When we turn to the literature of the thirteenth and fourteenth centuries, we find certain poets and literary scholars confronting a problem similar to that of the philosophers—how to mediate between divergent or conflicting traditions—and we find them attempting to resolve that problem by methods analogous to those of the philosophers.

The parallel development of different disciplines within a culture has sometimes been attributed to the direct influence of one upon the other. Such, for example, is the claim of Erwin Panofsky's study *Gothic Architecture and Scholasticism* (1951), which shows several ways in which the medieval architect could have absorbed the mental habits of logicians. More often it is the case, though, that there is no influence of one art upon the other, or else that scarcity of evidence makes it impossible to determine whether any direct relation existed. This is no handicap to scholarship. On the contrary, it may be an advantage, for where we observe no direct influence among the arts we are free to search for other causes which may give a more accurate picture of historical development than can be found in mechanical imitation. The historian Marc Bloch remarked that the most interesting similarities are those that "prove not to be explicable in terms of imitation . . . for they allow us to take a real step forward in the exciting search for causes." There appears to be no direct influence of late medieval skeptical philosophy on the literature of the period; certainly nothing of the kind can be shown for

Chaucer, whose reading was eclectic and often superficial, and of whose education almost nothing is known. Were one to follow far enough the network of habits, institutions, and events that constitute a culture, causal patterns would likely emerge. One would have to inquire, for instance, why the translation of Aristotle's work into Latin was delayed until the late twelfth century, and why it was done at that time; why the Church was unable or unwilling to enforce its early bans against Aristotle's work; what social and economic conditions generated the late medieval literary works Chaucer used as his sources; and whether these phenomena are not related through a set of common causes. Though these and similar questions are certainly answerable, it is beyond the scope of this study to answer them. Rather than discuss the origins of the structural and ideological similarities between philosophy and literature, I intend only to describe those similarities as the introduction to my study of the *House of Fame.*

The opening lines of the Prologue to Chaucer's *Legend of Good Women* provide a paradigm of the evolution of skeptical fideism, and also of some of its literary consequences. First the intellectual problem is stated: doctrinal authority requires assent to propositions for which no proof is possible.

> A thousand tymes have I herd men telle
> That ther ys joy in hevene and peyne in helle,
> And I acorde wel that it ys so;
> But, natheles, yet wot I wel also
> That ther nis noon dwellyng in this contree,
> That eyther hath in hevene or helle ybe,
> Ne may of hit noon other weyes witen,
> But as he hath herd seyd, or founde it writen;
> For by assay ther may no man it preve.
>
> (F, 1–9)

The Narrator hastens to reject the simple materialism that may spring from the desire for empirical evidence:

> But God forbede but men shulde leve
> Wel more thing then men han seen with ye!
> Men shal not wenen every thing a lye
> But yf himself yt seeth, or elles dooth;
> For, God wot, thing is never the lasse sooth,
> Thogh every wight ne may it nat ysee.
> Bernard the monk ne saugh nat all, pardee!
>
> *(F, 10–16)*

Some things, he argues, are to be accepted without direct proof. In the next lines the Narrator quietly shifts ground from metaphysical to historical matters, thus avoiding any outright statement about the role of religious authority. For want of absolute certainty about the past, the Narrator gives fideistic assent to traditional literary and historical sources:

> Than mote we to bokes that we fynde,
> Thurgh whiche that olde thinges ben in mynde,
> And to the doctrine of these olde wyse
> Yeve credence, in every skylful wise,
> That tellen of these olde appreved stories
> Of holynesse, of regnes, of victories,
> Of love, of hate, of other sondry thynges,
> Of whiche I may nat make rehersynges.
> And yf that olde bokes were aweye,
> Yloren were of remembraunce the keye.
> Wel ought us thanne honouren and beleve
> These bokes, there we han noon other preve.
>
> *(F, 17–28)*

The Narrator acknowledges that authority itself is not sufficient proof of a given proposition or event; but he maintains simultaneously that where no adequate proof is available, a "leap of faith" is required in order to avoid agnosticism. His procedure as a poet, then, will be to follow his sources faithfully:

> On bokes for to rede I me delyte,
> And to hem yeve I feyth and ful credence.
>
> *(F, 30–31)*

The credo is repeated at the beginning of the legend of Dido:

> Glorye and honour, Virgil Mantoan,
> Be to thy name! and I shal, as I can,
> Folwe thy lanterne, as thow gost byforn,
> How Eneas to Dido was forsworn.
>
> *(924–27)*

How limited a literary program this is, the *Legend of Good Women* itself illustrates. Despite the Narrator's affirmation of belief and his statement of intention, the poem is a patchwork of classical and contemporary material, of originals and translations. Virgil's story of Dido is freely adulterated with other versions—a liberty for which the Scots poet Gavin Douglas later took Chaucer severely to task. The *Legend of Good Women* shows theory and practice sharply at odds (in the Narrator's mind at least, if not necessarily in Chaucer's). An unswerving commitment to tradition cannot be maintained, since tradition is multivalent and contradictory. Whether Chaucer's defection from classical orthodoxy in the *Legend of Good Women* represents an attitude of irony toward his sources, or one of indecision, is not certain; in either case it points to the inadequacy of a Higden-like confidence in "fama diuturna."

The skeptical vision is also evident in *Troilus and Criseyde,* whose style and structure underscore the ambivalence of experience as well as of tradition. E. Talbot Donaldson has noticed Chaucer's technique of "deliberate mystification" in that work: a device by which various opinions and facts are purposely opened to doubt and never resolved.[1] Did Criseyde have children? Did she fall in love too quickly? Was Pandarus's role above reproach? As Donaldson remarks, "the narrator's explanations are even worse than his silences." Frequent puns intensify the deliberately equivocal effect of the poem's verbal texture. Besides such stylistic features (which reflect the confusing

---

1. See Donaldson's essay on *Troilus* in *Chaucer's Poetry*, pp. 965–80.

variety of material in the Troilus tradition itself), there is the mystery of "Lollius," whom Chaucer claims as the source of his work (1. 394; 5. 1653). Doubtless this was a mistake made in good faith, and Chaucer did think that there was a Lollius who wrote about the Trojan War.[2] But he could not have consulted such a work, as he claims to have done, nor does he mention his actual major source, the *Filostrato* of his contemporary, Giovanni Boccaccio. So that while he is not constrained to follow any single source faithfully, Chaucer must nevertheless justify his fiction by reference to some ancient authority. His practice in *Troilus* suggests some awareness that the truth of fiction is not always identical with that of history (especially since the latter can only rarely be determined); but the medieval habit of dependence on authority is still strong enough in Chaucer to overbalance the claims of poetic independence.

If the style of *Troilus* reveals the skepticism with which Chaucer approached literary tradition and human experience, it is the structure of the poem that displays the fideistic resolution—or, more accurately, the fideistic evasion—of contradiction. Various attitudes have been represented in the poem toward love, toward war, toward Criseyde. The last scene describes the ascent of Troilus's soul, after his death, to the eighth heavenly sphere; the hero is now a remote observer of the human events in which he had participated. From this vantage point Troilus perceives the vanity of earthly affairs in comparison with the bliss of afterlife:

> [he] fully gan despise
> This wrecched world, and held al vanite
> To respect of the pleyn felicite
> That is in hevene above . . .
> *(1816–19)*

---

2. On Lollius, see G. L. Kittredge, "Chaucer's Lollius," *Harvard Studies in Classical Philology* 28 (1917), and R. A. Pratt, "A Note on Chaucer's Lollius," *MLN* 65 (1950).

The introduction of a Christian perspective permits the author to address his audience with a direct admonition to abandon the "worldly vanyte" of love and to turn instead to Christ:

> And syn he best to love is, and most meke,
> What nedeth feynede loves for to seke?
>
> *(1847–48)*

Although no rational choice is made among the earthly alternatives presented in the poem, the problem of choice is transcended in this conclusion, to which any rational argument must be irrelevant.

One direction in which a skeptical approach to tradition might develop is suggested by a later treatment of the story of Troilus and Cressida: that of the Scots poet Robert Henryson in his *Testament of Cresseid* (c. 1492). Now, ironically, the literary authority is Chaucer. Henryson relates how on a winter's evening he

> tuik ane Quair, and left all uther sport,
> Writtin be worthie Chaucer glorious,
> Of fair Cresseid, and worthie Troilus.
>
> *(40–42)*

Despite his obvious respect for the English poet, Henryson goes on to ask, "Quha wait gif all that Chauceir wrait was trew?" Justified by doubt, Henryson takes down another book—apparently a fictitious source invented by himself for the occasion—which tells the "fatall destenie" of Cresseid that Henryson now proceeds to narrate. Even this second book, though, is guaranteed no historical authority:

> Nor I wait nocht gif this narratioun
> Be authoreist, or fenyeit of the new
> Be sum Poeit, throw his Inventioun . . . .
>
> *(65–67)*

Like Chaucer, Henryson defers to his audience's expectation that there is a respectable traditional source for his work, and, like Chaucer, he invents one. But Henryson, confronting an uncertain tradition, claims nothing for either his real source or his invented one. Instead, admitting that no certainty can be derived from any of his literary antecedents, he withdraws the assurance he had momentarily held out to his reader. Indeed the double irony of the "feigned" source is not only that its story was invented by a poet, but the very existence of the book itself was invented. Thus Henryson offers, as sources for his work, a well-known poem whose historical truth he deliberately casts into doubt, and another anonymous account that is plainly said to be of dubious historical worth. In doing so Henryson allows poetic invention an independent claim on our attention, even though this claim may not be identical with that of "authoreist" narrative.

We need not look to the fifteenth century for a more developed esthetic than Chaucer's, for Boccaccio's handling of the Troilus story in his *Filostrato* (1338) provides an instructive comparison. Boccaccio, like Chaucer, suppresses the names of his main sources, Benoit de Saint-Maure and Guido delle Colonne. Unlike Chaucer, though, Boccaccio invents no other authority to justify his own work. Instead the poem stands justified by the author's own motive, which is to create an emblem of his suffering at his mistress's departure:

> Meco adunque con sollecita cura comincai a rivolgere l'antiche storie, per trovare cui potessi verisimilmente fare scudo del mio segreto e amoroso dolore.
>
> *(Filostrato, Proem)*

Once the appropriate material is found among these "antiche storie," there is no question of verifying its truth, or of determining the reliability of one or another source— this despite the fact that Boccaccio's sources do explicitly and at some length take up the problem of veracity in the tradition. In the *Filostrato*, then, Boccaccio has already found the easiest solution to the problem of the credibility of sources. He ignores it, allowing his work an independent truth.

A like sense of literary integrity is evident in the *De-cameron* (1353), a collection of amusing stories placed in the sombre setting of plague-stricken Florence. In the conclusion to this work Boccaccio anticipates criticism of its bawdry, remarking that

> these stories are not told in a church, for churchly things should be treated with a pure mind, and spoken of in most reverent terms . . . Nor were they told in schools of philosophy, where propriety is expected of one, as anywhere else. No, they were not told by clerics or philosophers in any church or school, but in gardens and places of recreation and among youths and maidens.[3]

Each kind of discourse—sermon, logical treatise, or fiction—has, Boccaccio suggests, a purpose, an audience, and a style proper to it: none need intrude on the others. At first implied, now clearly asserted, the self-sufficiency of fiction seems to be a notion on which Boccaccio, unlike Chaucer, was able to rely throughout his career.

How was he able to do this? The rationale appears in a late work, its date supporting the observation that a poet's critical theory tends naturally to explain his own poetry. The *Genealogia Deorum Gentilium* (begun around 1355 and completed after 1371) is a compendium of mythological lore which Boccaccio compiled at the request of King Hugo of Cyprus. In the Prohemium to the *Genealogia* (a dedicatory letter to his patron), Boccaccio announces his intention to proceed objectively amidst a confusing mass of contradictory and improbable material.

> For fear you may think it my fault, I must not fail to explain that it is the Ancients who are to blame, not I, if you often meet in reading my work with statements that are so wide of the truth, so dis-

3. *The Decameron*, trans. Frances Winwar (New York, 1930), p. 663.

crepant, that you could never suppose them the utterances of philosophers, no, not even the inventions of rustics; other inconsistencies you will observe in their chronology. All these discrepancies and more I do not propose to reconcile or correct, unless they naturally submit to some order. I shall be satisfied merely to write down what I find and leave learned disputation to philosophers.[4]

In practice less disinterested, Boccaccio does in fact occasionally attempt to resolve a controversy. In discussing, for example, the question of "where poetry first dawned upon the world" (Bk. 14), he sets forth the argument for Hebrew, Babylonian, and Greek origins. After presenting the case for each, and after claiming to be unable to reach a decision, he arbitrarily concludes that Christian authority on the question must after all be considered definitive.

> With scholars thus at variance, and me unable to find evidence in ancient authors to support their theories, I cannot tell which to follow . . . . Nevertheless I cannot believe that the sublime effects of this great art were first bestowed upon Musaeus, or Linus, or Orpheus, however ancient. . . . Rather was it instilled into most sacred prophets, dedicated to God. For we read that Moses, impelled by what I take to be this poetic longing, at dictation of the Holy Ghost wrote the largest part of the Pentateuch not in prose but in heroic verse. . . . And I think the poets of the Gentiles in their poetry followed in the steps of these prophets; but whereas the holy men were filled with the Holy Ghost, and wrote under His impulse, the others·were prompted with mere energy of mind, whence such a one is called a "seer."[5]

---

4. Charles G. Osgood, trans., *Boccaccio on Poetry* (the Prologue and Books 14 and 15 of Boccaccio's *Genealogia Deorum Gentilium*), (Princeton, 1930), pp. 12–13.
5. Ibid., p. 46.

Here the solution, like Chaucer's in the Prologue to the *Legend of Good Women,* is to accept Christian authority where empirical or logical proof is lacking. But this is not, for Boccaccio, the scholar's best solution to the problem of credibility.

To circumvent conflicting arguments by way of Christian doctrine is a device adaptable to many kinds of writing. We have noticed it already in late medieval logic and natural philosophy, in Boccaccio's compilation of myths, and in some of Chaucer's poetry. It appears in other works as well, for example in the well-known *De Arte Honesti Amandi* (c. 1185) of Andreas Capellanus. Because this work helps to illustrate some difficulties in the method of escape through doctrine, I want briefly to analyze its structure. The treatise is an instructional manual written, according to its author, at the request of a young friend who had recently fallen in love. Its first two sections tell how the lover can best succeed in his aim, and describe the origin, practice, and ennobling effects of love. By contrast, the third section lists the many ill effects of love and presents a variety of moral, practical, and antifeminist arguments against it. To the reader the author correctly remarks in his conclusion, "Now this doctrine of ours, . . . will if carefully and faithfully examined seem to present two different points of view." Though his own point of view is evidently austere, Andreas does not rely on moral or practical arguments to dissuade his young friend from delights of the flesh. Instead he introduces a suprarational perspective in which sexual love is transformed into a metaphor for the climactic event of Christian faith:

> Pass by all the vanities of the world, so that when the Bridegroom cometh to celebrate the greater nuptials, and the cry ariseth in the night, you may be prepared to go forth to meet Him with your lamps filled and to go in with Him to the divine marriage. . . . Do not let worldly delight make you lie down in your sins, trusting to the youth of your

body and confident that the Bridegroom will be late, since, as He tells us himself, we know neither the day nor the hour.[6]

To such a perspective, rational argument can add nothing. Andreas's treatise suggests that reliance on Christian doctrine has the advantage of absolving the writer (and the reader) from choosing among conflicting arguments on the basis of evidence. The disadvantage of the method, though, are considerable. As historical method, it tends to minimize the importance of history; as a mode of argument it supersedes argument; as a literary principle it deprecates the independent value of the fictive world. No doubt aware of the deficiency of literary fideism, Boccaccio attempted to meet the problem of truth in fiction in Books 14 and 15 of the *Genealogia*. They constitute a defense of poetry some of whose arguments anticipate those of English Renaissance critics. Boccaccio's poetics is not, of course, based on classical theory but on the characteristically medieval critical method of symbolic or allegorical interpretation. In attempting to prove the independent validity of fiction, Boccaccio remains faithful to the original purpose of allegorical interpretation, which was to prove the independent validity of Christianity. One use of allegorical method was to adjust biblical improbabilities to the data of perceptible reality; another was to reconcile both the Old Testament and the classical literary tradition with Christian doctrine. The symbolic interpretation of Old Testament passages and of classical literature offered a way of mediating between authority and experience, or between conflicting authorities.

Boccaccio's interpretation of the mythical figure of Fama will illustrate the allegorical method. Fama was said to be the monstrous daughter of Earth, produced by Earth to avenge the death of her sons, the Titans, at the hands

6. *The Art of Courtly Love*, trans. John Jay Parry (New York, 1941), pp. 211–12.

of the gods. The meaning of this myth Boccaccio explains
as follows:

> Doubtless the stars do influence us. . . . And some-
> times they do things which seem to mortals to be
> done suddenly and ill-advisedly, as if from anger,
> as for instance when the just king, the blessed ruler,
> or the vigorous knight are brought to their death.
> . . . But what follows from this is that earth—that
> is, proud man, for we are all of earth—is angered by
> this. And to what is earth provoked? That it gives
> birth to fame, the avenger of future deaths. In other
> words, man does things because of which the fame
> of his name is established, so that when the gods
> kill him, the reputation of his virtues survives by
> the agency of fame.[7]

Symbolic interpretation opens the way to the complete
independence of fiction, for in asserting poetic intention
as the main standard of judgment, it renders irrelevant the
fact of improbability. The consequences of symbolic interpretation become clear in Book 15 of the *Genealogia*, where
fiction is distinguished from falsehood.

> Poetic fiction has nothing in common with any
> variety of falsehood, for it is not the poet's purpose
> to deceive anybody with his inventions; further-
> more, poetic fiction differs from a lie in that in most
> instances it bears not only no close resemblance to
> the literal truth, but no resemblance at all.[8]

The symbolic function of myth or fiction also exonerates
the poet from charges of doctrinal falsehood, for what is
unacceptable to Christian faith can be understood on the
level of figurative, not doctrinal, truth.

> Without question poets do say in their works that
> there are many gods, when there is but One. But
> they should not therefore be charged with false-

---

7. *Genealogiae Joannis Boccatii* . . . (Venice, 1511), Liber 1, cap. 10.
8. Osgood, *Boccaccio*, p. 63.

hood, since they neither believe nor assert it as fact, but only as a myth or fiction, according to their wont.[9]

Somewhat more complicated is the status of such fiction as epic, neither patently improbable nor historically true. Where the poet has achieved verisimilitude, can he be accused of deceit? Boccaccio refutes this objection with the notion of the exemplary value of fiction, and he includes in the realm of fictional truth that which might be or ought to be true.

> There is one kind of fiction very like the truth, which . . . is more like history than fiction, and which by ancient agreement of all peoples has been free from taint of falsehood. This is so in virtue of their consent from of old that anyone who could, might use it as an illustration in which the literal truth is not required, nor its opposite forbidden. And if one considers the function of the poet already described, clearly poets are not constrained by this bond to employ literal truth on the surface of their inventions.[10]

By way of allegorical and exemplary interpretation, then, Boccaccio has arrived at a statement of the independence of fiction from both history and Christian doctrine. The foundation of that independence is a distinction between the kinds of truth contained in each kind of writing. One can appreciate the liberating effect of such a distinction, for it frees the poet to commit himself to a source, to a tradition, or to a poetic statement regardless of its doctrinal or historical validity.

Despite its benefits, the distinction between kinds of truth was one which Chaucer was unable fully to accept as the basis for literary practice. The *House of Fame* shows that while Chaucer felt the dilemma which made the separation of truths necessary, still he preferred to transcend

9. Ibid., p. 65.
10. Ibid., p. 63.

the choice between traditions rather than to commit himself wholeheartedly to a single intellectual tradition or consistent point of view. He was, profoundly, a Laodicean, despite the late Professor Loomis's effort to clear him of that charge.[11] Understandably, Chaucer's reluctance to commit himself troubles some readers; yet that same pluralistic impulse also generates the irony and richness of perception that constitute Chaucer's main appeal. Chaucer's stance both pleased and troubled Matthew Arnold, who granted his art "largeness, freedom, shrewdness, benignity" but denied it "high seriousness." The *House of Fame* takes us to what, for the poet, is the heart of pluralism: tradition itself. Not incoherency but incongruity is characteristic of the *House of Fame;* indeed it is its subject, because incongruity is the essence of fame.

11. See Roger Sherman Loomis, "Was Chaucer a Laodicean?" *Essays and Studies in Honor of Carleton Brown* (New York, 1940), pp. 129–48.

4

Dreams and Truth

God turne us every drem to goode!
For hyt is wonder, be the roode,
To my wyt, what causeth swevenes
Eyther on morwes or on evenes . . . .

The House of Fame, 1–4

As a short compendium of medieval dream theory, the Proem to the *House of Fame* is a suitable induction to a dream-vision, even if its volume of information leaves us, with the Narrator, overwhelmed. The Narrator's presentation of the terminology, causes, and effects of dreams does more, though, than prepare us for the vision to follow. It represents the first stage in a process of expanding consciousness. The second is developed in Book 1, where the Narrator will retell at length the well-known story of Aeneas, and where he will confront the problem of conflicting heroic obligations. In Book 2 the Narrator will travel through the universe on his way to Fame's palace. In that section of the poem his interest will be the nature of the supraterrestrial environment: its landmarks, its laws, its effect on the cosmic traveller. The poem takes us, therefore, from psychology through history to cosmology, from microcosm to macrocosm, from the world of the mind through the world of men to the created world at large. This structural movement echoes one metaphysical structure by which men have linked themselves to the universe,

36

for according to the elemental theory of creation, man and the universe are composed of the same elements and governed by the same natural laws. The notion of correspondence between microcosm and macrocosm, derived from Platonic tradition and expressed in graphic and literary art throughout the Middle Ages, was well known to Chaucer from numerous sources.[1] In the *House of Fame*, the movement from inner to outer world supplies a changing, expanding backdrop for symbolic action. In each setting—psyche, history, cosmos—the Narrator confronts a set of alternatives, each of which is defined in terms of its literary tradition. Among these alternatives the Narrator is each time unable to choose, but he is able to transcend his indecision with a fideistic appeal to God or to Christ. Narrative material, then, changes in a pattern of progressive enlargement, very like the circles in water that form the basis of the Eagle's argument in Book 2. And, as with those same circles, the center remains constant, for the variation in narrative material causes no alteration in the overall structure of each episode.

It is appropriate, in the Proem to a dream-vision, for the author to introduce some remarks about the value of dreams. To do so amounts to an esthetic justification for the work to follow; for if the dream is acknowledged to be at least potentially a vehicle of truth, then the dream-vision frame may be considered to add authenticity. The dream-vision provides other advantages as well.[2] It permits the writer to treat questions which man cannot hope to answer by reason alone but which may require an epiphany or an

1. Among them the *De Mundi Universitate* of Bernard Silvestris, Prosa 13; Alanus de Insulis, *De Planctu Naturae*, Prosa 3; *Roman de la Rose*, 19021 ff. Other medieval sources of the microcosm theory are given in Jean Seznec, *The Survival of the Pagan Gods* (New York, 1953), p. 65; A. C. Crombie traces it to Plato's *Timaeus* and subsequent Stoic astrology, *Medieval Science*, 1: 18. See also E. de Bruyne, *Études d'Esthétique Médiévale* (Bruges, 1945), 2: 355–56.

2. For some of the following points about the dream-vision frame I am indebted to Francis X. Newman's dissertation, "Somnium: Medieval Theories of Dreaming and the Form of Vision Poetry" (Princeton, 1963), chapter 5.

oracular answer. As a possibly supernatural phenomenon the device tends to absolve the writer from direct responsibility for statements that may be made in the work. It involves the reader more intimately than straightforward narrative, for the reader becomes both interpreter of the dream and judge of its truth. Moreover, since anyone is capable of dreaming, the reader can legitimately expect to participate in or benefit from the exemplary action portrayed in the vision—the dream-vision is anything but an elitist form. Finally, the dream-vision may serve as a device for disarming the literal-minded critic who might object to the presentation of improbable events in a context of waking life.

Since dreams were not accepted as uniformly valid, most dream-visions in medieval literature begin with an assertion of the truth of dreams in general, or at least of the particular dream about to be told. One of the best-known of these statements occurs at the beginning of the *Roman de la Rose*. I give it in Chaucer's translation:

> Many men sayn that in swevenynges
> Ther nys but fables and lesynges;
> But men may some swevenes sen
> Whiche hardely that false ne ben,
> But afterward ben apparaunt.
> This may I drawe to warraunt
> An author that hight Macrobes,
> That halt nat dremes false ne lees,
> But undoth us the avysioun
> That whilom mette kyng Cipioun.
> And whoso saith or weneth it be
> A jape, or elles nycete,
> To wene that dremes after falle,
> Let whoso lyste a fol me calle.
> For this trowe I, and say for me,
> That dremes signifiaunce be
> Of good and harm to many wightes,

That dremen in her slepe a-nyghtes
Ful many thynges covertly,
That fallen after al openly.

(A, 1–20)

Such assertions of the validity of dreams form a branch of
the extremely common "truth topos" found in many kinds
of medieval literature.[3] The invention of historical or literary sources and the protestation of faithful reportage are
other typical means of justifying the literary work.

That Chaucer knew the traditional uses of the truth
apparatus is shown not only in his translation of the
Roman de la Rose but in his use of that apparatus for his
own original works. Two passages from the *Canterbury
Tales* will illustrate Chaucer's familiarity with the tradition. In both of these passages, the justification rests on a
mimetic theory of art. The first, from the General Prologue,
absolves the poet from any suspicion of "vileynye" in
adopting a low or uneducated style. Such, the Narrator
claims, is the style in which his fellow-pilgrims spoke, and
to use a more elevated style would be untrue to the event.
Besides, even Christ used a low style in the Scriptures.

But first I pray yow, of youre courteisye,
That ye n'arette it nat my vileynye,
Thogh that I pleynly speke in this mateere,
To telle yow hir wordes and hir cheere,
Ne thogh I speke hir wordes proprely.
For this ye knowen al so wel as I,
Whoso shal telle a tale after a man,

3. See, for example, Nicole Margival, *Le Dit de la Panthère d'Amours*
(c. 1295), lines 41-43, ed. H. Todd, *SATF* 16 (1883); *Mum and the Soth-
segger*, lines 873 and 1309–1333, ed. M. Day and Robert Steele, EETS 199
(1936); *Piers Plowman*, Passus 7, B-text, lines 151 ff. The classic biblical
examples used to prove the validity of dreams were Joseph and Daniel.
According to Robert Manning's manual *Handling Synne*, 390 ff., these
illustrate two special types of revelation, caused respectively by God's
warning and by too much study. On the tradition of the truth apparatus generally, see H. L. Levy, "As Myn Auctor Seyth," *Medium Aevum*
12 (1943).

He moot reherce as ny as ever he kan
Everich a word, if it be in his charge,
Al speke he never so rudelich and large,
Or ellis he moot telle his tale untrewe,
Or feyne thyng, or fynde wordes newe.
He may nat spare, althogh he were his brother;
He moot as wel seye o word as another.
Crist spak hymself ful brode in hooly write,
And wel ye woot no vileynye is it.
Eek Plato seith, whoso that kan hym rede,
The wordes moote be cosyn to the dede.

(GP 725–42)

The second passage, from the Miller's Prologue, also uses
the argument that the poet chronicles real events:

What sholde I moore seyn, but this Millere
He nolde his wordes for no man forbere,
But tolde his cherles tale in his manere.
M'athynketh that I shal reherce it heere.
And therfore every gentil wight I preye,
For Goddes love, demeth nat that I seye
Of yvel entente, but for I moot reherce
Hir tales alle, be they bettre or werse,
Or elles falsen som of my mateere.

(3167–75)

Of course the irony in both apologies is that the reported
event itself is a fiction (though one with analogues in real
life), so that the low style is as artful and "feyned" as any
other could be.

In both of Chaucer's other dream-visions, the dream is
authenticated by means of a book which the Narrator reads
just before falling asleep. The content of each dream is
supposedly generated by the book: a "romaunce" of Ceyx
and Halcyon in the *Book of the Duchess,* and "Tullyus of
the Drem of Scipioun" in the *Parliament of Fowls.*

Despite his awareness of the conventional certification
of literary truth, and his use of it elsewhere, in the *House*

of Fame Chaucer chooses to ignore it. Indeed he subverts it, undermining the reader's inclination to believe the dream that is about to be told.

The fifty-line sentence that opens and constitutes nearly all of the Proem is a plethora of contradictory information about dreams:

> As yf folkys complexions
> Make hem dreme of reflexions;
> Or ellys thus, as other sayn,
> For to gret feblenesse of her brayn,
> By abstinence, or by seknesse,
> Prison, stewe, or gret distresse,
> Or ellys by dysordynaunce
> Of naturel acustumaunce,
> That sum man is to curious
> In studye, or melancolyous,
> Or thus, so inly ful of drede,
> That no man may hym bote bede;
> Or elles that devocion
> Of somme, and contemplacion
> Causeth such dremes ofte. . . .
>
> *(21–35)*

One's first reaction to this extended *dubitatio* may be amusement, but the cumulative impression created by its piled-up clauses is of futility: it is hopeless to think of ascertaining the truth about dreams. The juxtaposition of so many opposed theories shows that too much information is as fatal to certainty as too little. Faced with this confusion, the reader can only repeat with the Narrator the wish that frames the Proem, "God turn us every dream to good!" (lines 1, 57–58). Since there is no rational way of choosing among theories, choice is abandoned; so is prediction, and the outcome of all dreams is left with God. The Narrator transcends given alternatives in a fideistic appeal to the highest authority—a suprarational authority. It is a structural pattern that remains constant throughout the work. And if the tone of the Proem is jocular or its narrative material frivolous, the Narrator's attention will soon be directed toward weightier matters. Besides eliminating any possibility of certainty about the truth of dreams in general, Chaucer further omits from both Proem and Invocation any reference to the validity of his particular vision. It is not said to be the result of any event in real life or of a special inspiration, nor is any claim made that this vision can in turn illuminate real life. Unlike most writers, Chaucer does not in the *House of Fame* encourage his audience to believe what it is about to hear. Nevertheless he does urge his audience to approach the work in good faith, calling down a curse on those who refuse to do so.

> And he that mover ys of al
> That is and was and ever shal,
> So yive hem joye that hit here . . .
> And sende hem al that may hem plese,
> That take hit wel and skorne hyt noght,
> Ne hyt mysdemen in her thoght
> Thorgh malicious entencion.
> And whoso thorgh presumpcion,
> Or hate, or skorn, or thorgh envye,
> Dispit, or jape, or vilanye,
> Mysdeme hyt, pray I Jesus God
> That (dreme he barefot, drem he shod),
> That every harm that any man
> Hath had, syth the world began,
> Befalle hym therof . . . .
>
> *(81–101)*

This is more than the conventional opening topos against envious detractors, though it does participate in that tradition.[4] It represents an important shift in emphasis, for the reader is invited to judge ("demen") rather than required

4. The envious detractors topos has a particularly illustrious tradition, stretching from an inscription by Tiglath Pileser's scribe (see *The Gilgamesh Epic and Old Testament Parallels*, ed. Alexander Heidel, p. 139) to Rabelais' Prologue to *Gargantua*. It appears in the prologues to Einhard's *Life of Charlemagne*, Alanus's *Anticlaudianus*, Marie's lai

to believe. The question of truth is left aside entirely—an omission that can hardly be accidental when the point is so prominent a feature in medieval literature, especially in the dream-vision form which the *House of Fame* represents. Although the argument is made partly *ex silentio*, the Invocation clearly suggests a nascent awareness of the self-sufficiency of fiction. Chaucer does not, in this poem, present himself as the chronicler of real events, nor does he claim the reader's belief. Further, Chaucer is sufficiently skeptical about his traditional material to undercut it with irony, in the pointed juxtaposition of contradictory theories. He undercuts it again in altering the traditional May date of the courtly dream-vision to December 10 (line 63).

The Narrator's bitter curse on his hypothetical detractors eliminates still another traditional source of security for the audience: the poet's moral character and his elevated purpose. Another widely used device for opening a poem was the charity topos, in which the poet claimed his motive to be the edification of his audience through presentation of exemplary action.[5] The act of writing becomes itself a charitable act, through which the poet hopes to gain his heavenly reward. In the *House of Fame*, however, far from claiming any virtue to offset his vindictiveness, the Narrator reinforces the bitterness of his curse with this stubborn last remark:

> This prayer shal he have of me;
> I am no bet in charyte!
>
> *(107–8)*

With the work deliberately stripped of any external support from literary tradition or the Narrator's own character,

---

Guigemar, and Chaucer's *Astrolabe*. F. Tupper traces the topos through the seventeenth century, "The Envy Theme in Prologues and Epilogues," *JEGP* 16 (1917). James A. Work suggests that the passage in the *House of Fame* echoes the great curse of excommunication, "Echoes of the Anathema in Chaucer," *PMLA* 47 (1932).

5. For the charity topos, see Chretien de Troyes, *Erec et Enide*, 1–18; Marie de France, Prologue to the *Lais*, 1–8; *La Venjance Alixandre*, Laisse 1; *Aymeri de Narbonne*, Laisses 1–3; and *Le Dit de l'Unicorne*.

our trust will have to derive from the quality of the work itself.

The problem foreshadowed in the Proem and Invocation is that fame or tradition, being all-inclusive, provides too many answers; it encourages not certainty but doubt. Uncertainty about facts, whether historical or scientific, is disturbing to the scholar, but more disturbing to the poet must be uncertainty about his own position. In what ways can the poet use authorities whose authority he doubts? And if the poet's skepticism toward traditional material has subverted his old role as truth-teller, what amenities will govern the new and more difficult relation between poet and audience? These problems Chaucer does not fully resolve in the *House of Fame,* though he takes some tentative steps toward doing so. We must look ahead to *Troilus and Criseyde* for the integration of skeptical vision with literary practice.

The dream-vision frame is significant in relation to such questions. Chaucer's irony removes the traditional authenticating function of dream-lore so that it can no longer certify the validity of the work, and his silence about the real-life circumstances of the dream deprives us of a peg on which to suspend disbelief. Cut off from the usual supports of theoretical authority and historical fact, the composition, like the dream, becomes a free-floating quantum of creative or psychic energy, subject to good or evil influences and capable in turn of exercising a good or an evil influence on its audience. The Narrator requires protection as dreamer and as poet, for if neither dream-theory nor literary tradition offers certain truth, then neither dreaming nor writing offers any security of role. That the Narrator's position as dreamer and as poet is the same suggests that the dream is not only analogous to the composition but may be a metaphor for it—or, more accurately, for the poetic conception embodied in the work. The process of dreaming becomes nearly synonymous with the creative act.

The classical invocations to the three books of the *House of Fame* suggest the symbolic relation of dream to composition. The first invocation asks Morpheus, god of sleep, for the power to tell the dream correctly:

> And to this god, that I of rede,
> Prey I that he wol me spede
> My sweven for to telle aryght,
> Yf every drem stonde in his myght.
>
> (77–80)

The connection seems straightforward and evident: because the poem relates a dream, the poem cannot be "true" unless the dream is accurately recounted. Yet when we recall the skeptical attitude toward dreams in the Proem, we realize that even to tell the dream "aryght" is no guarantee of its ultimate truth. In the second and third invocations the Narrator speaks more directly of his attempt to recreate a particular image:

> O Thought, that wrot al that I mette,
> And in the tresorye hit shette
> Of my brayn, now shal men se
> Yf any vertu in the be,
> To tellen al my drem aryght.
> Now kythe thyn engyn and myght!
>
> (II, 523–28)

> And yif, devyne vertu, thow
> Wilt help me to shewe now
> That in myn hed ymarked ys—
> Loo, that is for to menen this,
> The Hous of Fame for to descryve—
> Thou shalt se me go as blyve
> Unto the nexte laure y see,
> And kysse it, for hyt is thy tree.
>
> (III, 1101–8)

Here the poetic conception is described in terms that might apply either to a dream or to creative inspiration, inasmuch as both are forms of intense mental activity, both are possibly the action of an external power ("vertu"), and both produce images that may require interpretation. Whatever its source, the poetic idea has to be translated into communicable form. Here the possibility of error can enter the creative process, for if the artistic form of the idea does not adequately represent the original conception, the work will be "false." The three classical invocations express the Narrator's desire to communicate what is in some sense accurate or true. Although "truth" is not clearly defined in the *House of Fame,* Chaucer's skepticism about dreams and his undercutting of traditional authority imply that this truth does not necessarily belong to the class of ascertainable facts. In his invocations Chaucer seems tentatively to define truth in fiction as fidelity to a poetic idea ("That in myn hed ymarked ys"). One might expect such a notion to dispel Chaucer's anxiety about truth in poetry. But a further difficulty remains, for even such a liberal notion of literary truth cannot guarantee the validity of inspiration itself—which, like the dream, may be delusive. Both imagination and the dream require special guidance, and this the Narrator invokes at the end of Book 1 in his prayer asking protection from "fantome and illusion" (see below, chapter 6).

We have seen how a superabundance of information about dreams led Chaucer to dispense with certain conventions of the dream-vision form: he cannot assert in good faith the absolute validity of this or any other dream. The traditional bond between poet and reader is at least partly severed, fair judgment replacing belief as the appropriate audience response. But a profusion of authorities existed in many other areas than dream-lore, and Chaucer's reading of contradictory literary texts was, as we shall see, an important source of his concern with poetic truth. His choice of one of the most famous stories in the medieval tradition —that of Aeneas and Dido—permitted him to explore that problem in terms of the different moral imperatives defined by different literary authorities. His method in Book 1, where the story of Aeneas is told, is not substantially changed from his method in the Proem, though it is on a larger scale and its tone, no longer comical, is appropriate to the problem of heroic choice.

5
Dido and Aeneas

The setting of the first book of the *House of Fame* is the Temple of Venus, on whose walls the Narrator finds portrayed the story of Dido and Aeneas. During the Middle Ages "every schoolboy" knew that story, or at least every well-read person knew it, whether in Virgil's *Aeneid*, in Ovid's "Epistle of Dido," in a vernacular romance or chronicle, in an encyclopedic compilation, or as an exemplary anecdote in a vernacular love-poem.[1] The two earliest versions known to Chaucer were the *Aeneid* and the seventh epistle ("Dido Aeneae") in Ovid's *Heroides*, to which sources he sends his audience:

> Rede Virgile in Eneydos
> Or the Epistle of Ovyde . . . .
> *(378–79)*

Both the Virgilian and the Ovidian versions of Dido and Aeneas are used in the Narrator's account of what he sees in the Temple of Venus, though the differences between them are not easily reconciled. In the former, for instance, it is plainly the hero's obligation to leave his mistress; in the latter he is blamed as a traitor. For the critic to try to reconcile such differences in the interest of "organic unity" or "unified point of view" would represent a misreading of

---

1. Some representative texts are the *Ilias Latina* of Simon Aurea Capra, ed. A. Boutemy, *Scriptorium* 1 (1946–47); the Old French romance *Enéas*, ed. J. Salverda de Grave (Halle, 1891); the *Roman de la Rose*, 13173–210; Chretien's *Erec et Enide*, 5289–98; Guillaume de Machaut's "Le Jugement dou Roy de Navarre," 2095 ff.

the poem, as well as a misunderstanding of medieval esthetics. The structural principle of the *House of Fame* is not the unity we tend to value so highly, in which subject matter and plot development provide the major statement of meaning. Rosamund Tuve remarked of Renaissance poetry that "A poem's content is not its use; it is the first choice of instrument made by the poet."[2] That is equally true of medieval poetry, in which meaning is likely to be developed through structural repetition. Explicit content, then, may be less central to meaning than method or structure, and that structure may be grasped at various points in the work. An analogy from architectural criticism will illustrate this principle:

> The infinity of movement which is macrocosmically expressed in the architectural structure as a whole expresses itself microcosmically in every smallest detail of the building. Every individual detail is, in itself, a world of bewildering activity and infinity, a world which repeats in miniature, but with the same means, the expression of the whole. . . . The crown of a pinnacle is a cathedral in miniature, and anyone who has sunk himself in the ingenious chaos of a tracery can here experience on a small scale the same thrill in logical formalism as he experiences in the building system as a whole. The unity of the will to form, with its unfailing accomplishment, is astounding.[3]

That Chaucer, in Book 1 of the *House of Fame*, allows the two classical versions of Aeneas to stand in such blatant

2. Rosamund Tuve, *Elizabethan and Metaphysical Imagery* (Chicago, 1947), p. 110.
3. Wilhelm Worringer, *Form in Gothic*, tran. Sir Herbert Read from *Formenprobleme der Gothik* (1910), (New York, 1964), p. 66. Several critics have already noticed the architectonic character of Chaucer's poetry; see Wolfgang Clemen, *Chaucer's Early Poetry* (London, 1963), p. 10, and Robert O. Payne, *The Key of Remembrance* (New Haven, 1963), p. 121. The analogy between architectural and poetic structure is drawn by Robert Jordan, *Chaucer and the Shape of Creation* (Cambridge, Mass., 1967), p. xi. See also D. W. Robertson, *A Preface to Chaucer* (Princeton, 1963), pp. 282–84.

contradiction should, I think, alert us to another purpose than that of retelling a famous story. Chaucer is not usually a careless craftsman; if his intention had been simply to illustrate Dido's fall into bad repute, he could easily have confined himself to the Ovidian view, as he would do (despite his disclaimers to the contrary) in the *Legend of Good Women*. The story of Dido and Aeneas is useful for the *House of Fame* precisely because its tradition is dual. Chaucer's treatment of the story repeats his treatment of dream-lore in the Proem, with, as we shall see, similar consequences for structure and style.

The episode begins with a paraphrase of the opening lines of the *Aeneid* which, like the original, calls attention to Aeneas's final destination. The Narrator finds a brass inscription which reads,

> "I wol now singen, yif I kan,
> The armes, and also the man
> That first cam, thurgh his destinee,
> Fugityf of Troy contree,
> In Itayle, with ful moche pyne
> Unto the strondes of Lavyne."
>
> *(143–48)*

The hero's purpose is referred to again when the Narrator describes how Creusa appeared to Aeneas during the sack of Troy; she

> Bad hym to flee the Grekes host,
> And seyde he moste unto Itayle,
> As was hys destinee, sauns faille.
> *(186–88)*

In the first section of Chaucer's narrative, the attitude toward Aeneas is distinctly sympathetic. He is recognizably the Virgilian hero, known for piety and familial devotion. The Narrator recounts, for instance, how Aeneas

> took his fader, Anchises,
> And bar hym on hys bak away,

> Cryinge, "Allas! and welaway!"
> The which Anchises in hys hond
> Bar the goddes of the lond,
> Thilke that unbrende were.
>   And I saugh next, in al thys fere,
> How Creusa, daun Eneas wif,
> Which that he lovede as hys lyf,
> And hir yonge sone Iulo,
> And eke Askanius also,
> Fledden eke with drery chere
> That hyt was pitee for to here . . . .
>   (168–80)

In this part of the story Aeneas is not held responsible for seducing Dido. The question of initiative in the love affair is left unclear, and we are told only that Venus

> made Eneas so in grace
> Of Dido, quene of that contree,
> That, shortly for to tellen, she
> Becam hys love, and let him doo
> Al that weddynge longeth too.
>   (240–44)

So far the story has been (with minor exceptions) a fairly accurate summary of the first three books of the *Aeneid* and part of the fourth.

At the moment when Dido makes Aeneas "hir lyf, hir love, hir lust, hir lord," an abrupt shift in the Narrator's attitude toward Aeneas marks the transition from the epic presentation of the love affair to the sentimental. It will be remembered that Virgil's Dido, confronting her lover with his planned departure, indulges in a shrewish, nearly hysterical tirade in which she does not refrain from sarcasm and vindictiveness. Aeneas, though restrained, is said (if not shown) to be fully sympathetic to her distress (4. 393–95). In Ovid's epistle, however, Dido is loving, tender, and pathetic. Since the work is written in her voice rather than in that of an omniscient narrator, the poet can easily manipulate the reader's emotional response. Ovid's Dido represents Aeneas as wholly unmoved by her emotion, as a traitor who abandoned his first wife, Creusa, and who will now abandon Dido herself despite the fact that she may be with child (a detail invented by Ovid in explicit contradiction of the Virgilian text). The Ovidian attitude, closer than the epic to medieval courtly sentiment, became usual in vernacular literature. It is a tradition which permits the Narrator to be overwhelmed with sympathy for Dido. Accordingly, Aeneas is transformed at this point into a calculating seducer of women.

> Allas! what harm doth apparence,
> Whan hit is fals in existence!
> For he to hir a traytour was;
> Wherfore she slow hirself, allas!
> Loo, how a woman doth amys
> To love him that unknown ys!
> For, be Cryste, lo, thus it fareth:
> "Hyt is not al gold that glareth."
> For also browke I wel myn hed,
> Ther may be under godlyhed
> Kevered many a shrewed vice.
> Therfore be no wight so nyce,
> To take a love oonly for chere,
> Or speche, or for frendly manere,
> For this shal every woman fynde,
> That som man, of his pure kynde,
> Wol shewen outward the fayreste,
> Tyl he have caught that what him leste;
> And thanne wol he causes fynde,
> And swere how that she ys unkynde,
> Or fals, or privy, or double was.
> Al this seye I be Eneas
> And Dido, and hir nyce lest,
> That loved al to sone a gest;
> Therfore I wol seye a proverbe,
> That "he that fully knoweth th'erbe

> May saufly leye hit to his yë";
> Withoute drede, this ys no lye.
>   But let us speke of Eneas,
> How he betrayed hir, allas!
> And lefte hir ful unkyndely.
>
> *(265–95)*

That Chaucer is aware of the overt sentimentality of this view of the story is betrayed by his rhetoric in the thirty lines above and in the forty-six lines immediately following, which contain Dido's plaint. Had Chaucer intended us to identify the Narrator's point of view here with his own (as some critics have done[4]) he would surely have used his skill to better effect. Most of the lines quoted above are sententious, if not directly proverbial, but these moral sentences are not justified by the story we have already been told. As far as we can see, Aeneas hides no "shrewd vice." Chaucer gives us no reason to think that Aeneas's intention was to seduce Dido, or that he attributed any fault to her in justification of his departure. Moreover, when at the end of the expostulation above, the Narrator declares that the time has come to speak of Aeneas, he proceeds instead to report Dido's lengthy complaint and ignores Aeneas altogether. A similar lapse occurs further on when the Narrator says that for the sake of brevity he will omit all that Dido wrote before she died; instead he provides a series of amplificatory exempla of false lovers which extends the story another forty-three lines. This sort of obvious narrative incompetence is a characteristic ironic device with Chaucer, appearing in the *Tale of Sir Thopas* and in many of the *Legends of Good Women*. It signals a parodic intention, or at the very least a divergence between Narrator and poet.

---

4. See, for instance, J. A. W. Bennett, *Chaucer's Book of Fame* (Oxford, 1968), p. 38: "All of Chaucer's sympathies, even while he shows her folly, are with Dido." And Clemen, *Chaucer's Early Poetry*, pp. 80–87, consistently identifies the Narrator with Chaucer himself. A salutary antidote to this approach is E. T. Donaldson's seminal essay "Chaucer the Pilgrim," *PMLA* 69 (1954): 928–36.

Apart from the general inapplicability of the Narrator's moral sentiments, the stylistic effect of this series of homely sententiae is parodic. It emerges as inflated style, not high style, an anticipation of the Eagle's well-meant pomposity in Book 2. Dido's complaint, it is true, is free of such bombast as is found in the Narrator's expostulation, but the lament is equally inappropriate to the narrative. Dido deplores at length (300–310) the fickleness of men and their desire for many lovers, even while it is clear that an historical mission, not another woman, draws Aeneas from her. She protests her innocence and good intentions, as if the departure could be interpreted as a form of revenge. She places all responsibility for her suffering on Aeneas, even though the burden of desire seems to have been hers from the beginning. In the light of this pervasive lack of logic, Dido's use of several terms of scholastic debate ("conclusyon," "determynen," "diffynen") in the last three lines of her plaint is the more ironically pointed.

Another reversal in the Narrator's attitude toward Aeneas occurs after he has given seven examples of other false lovers, all taken from Ovid's *Heroides*. At this point the attempt is made to pardon Aeneas.

> But to excusen Eneas
> Fullyche of al his grete trespas,
> The book seyth Mercurie, sauns fayle,
> Bad hym goo into Itayle,
> And leve Auffrikes regioun,
> And Dido and hir faire toun.
>
> (427–32)

The passage seems unconvincing after Dido's hyperbolic complaint. It is further weakened because it follows the event whose motivation it is supposed to supply, and because the Narrator relies on "the book" instead of providing direct personal comment. But the passage does not conclude the story; rather it is a transitional return to the epic material. The remainder of the narrative rapidly summarizes the last eight books of the *Aeneid*, once more stressing the hero's qualities of piety, devotion to family, and martial achievement.

> And also sawgh I how Sybile
> And Eneas, besyde an yle,
> To helle wente, for to see
> His fader, Anchyses the free. . . .
> Tho saugh I grave al the aryvayle
> That Eneas had in Itayle;
> And with kyng Latyne hys tretee
> And alle the batayles that hee
> Was at hymself, and eke hys knyghtis,
> Or he had al ywonne his ryghtis;
> And how he Turnus reft his lyf,
> And wan Lavina to his wyf;
> And alle the mervelous signals
> Of the goddys celestials . . . .
>
> *(439–60)*

The narrative ends with Aeneas rightfully established in Latium and, as in Virgil's epic, once again favored by the gods:

> For Jupiter took of hym cure
> At the prayer of Venus . . . .
> *(464–65)*

In Chaucer's version of the legend, then, we find the Ovidian love story framed in the larger context of Virgilian epic. Chaucer's inclusion of both sources suggests that Aeneas cannot be judged to be entirely right or entirely wrong. Upon that complexity, in which we recognize a permanent feature of life, depends, after all, the power of the legend. The *Aeneid* offers, of course, a stronger case for duty, presenting Aeneas as founder of the Roman Empire and devoting only one book of twelve to the love story. Ovid, confining himself wholly to Dido's case, tries to persuade his readers to the alternative view. In the Temple of

Venus, Chaucer's Narrator finds both values existing in an apparently stable equilibrium—as they exist in the tradition itself—and the Narrator is inclined to sympathize with Dido. Yet we ought not to allow our own antiheroic sentiments to obscure the structural function of the Narrator's response, for it is the Narrator's peculiarly impressionable character that allows Chaucer to introduce the Ovidian-courtly attitude. To have included it is neither an esthetic flaw nor capitulation to popular feeling. It is, on the contrary, a necessary part of the dialectic which balances Dido's claims against those of the hero. Indeed, if lines are to be counted, it will be found that the two points of view are very nearly evenly balanced.

Although the moral and esthetic problems posed by the legend of Dido and Aeneas are not simply reducible to a "true" position versus a false one, truth is nonetheless at the core of Chaucer's interest in the legend. In Dido's lament and the passage immediately following it (297–395), the word "true" and its variants appear five times, each time evoking several shades of meaning. There is "troth," the personal contractual relation which Dido mistakenly assumes; there is "piety"; there is "veracity." But the irony in Dido's insistence on truth as personal faith is that the heroic point of view must acknowledge a different definition. Though Chaucer does not use the word "troth" to denote the hero's commitment to his destiny, he does include the perspective of Aeneas's historical mission. Aeneas is burdened with his past and his future, so that to break his involuntary commitment would be a breach of troth indeed. This is Virgil's truth, but it is not Ovid's.

This paradox makes the story of Dido and Aeneas an appropriate introduction to a voyage to Fame's palace. It is not only that Aeneas is famous, but that he is famous in a particular way. What distinguishes his story from many others is its inherent ambivalence, for if the "pius" Aeneas was authorized by the literary canon, so was the traitor. What profounder comment on the nature of fame could there be than a tradition which shows the very essence of fame to be its utter disregard for the values it transmits? Give fame an upper-case initial, and you are half-way to Book 3 of the *House of Fame*, where the lesson is repeated through the means of personification allegory. The relevance of the legend of Dido and Aeneas is not to be found in its specific content, but in the exemplary value of the tradition itself.

In the Temple of Venus, then, the Narrator encounters more than a well-known love story, for his experience there duplicates Chaucer's experience as a poet. Were Chaucer fully convinced that fiction is independent of historical truth, a dual tradition would pose no difficulty: it could simply be ignored in the creation of his own version of "truth." Were he persuaded that the older tradition must be true, he could dispense with Ovid. As it is, Chaucer grants the validity of conflicting truths and confronts the problem with no way of deciding between them. No rational way, that is, and there is nothing in the Temple of Venus that can help him. But the adventure of Book 1 does not end on that doleful agnostic note. Though no choice can be made in the exclusively literary terms that have been established, to transcend the given terms of choice is the purpose of the Narrator's prayer at the end of Book 1.

6

Phantom

N either the iconography of the Temple of Venus nor the story told there is unusual in medieval literary tradition: sources for both were abundant in a number of well-known works. Less familiar than the Temple, though, is the landscape surrounding it: an extensive sand desert devoid of any sign of life, whether "toun, or hous, or tree,/ Or bush, or grass, or eryd lond." When the Narrator steps from the Temple to find himself alone in this wilderness, he utters a brief bewildered prayer:

> "O Christ! . . . that art in blysse,
> Fro fantome and illusion
> Me save!"
>
> *(492–94)*

These words mark a critical point in the narrative. The desert, as I have already noted, is an unusual feature in a medieval dream-vision, for the traditional locus is a luxuriant garden or wood watered by a clear stream and full of small wildlife. With its biblical and Dantesque overtones, so at odds with the lightness of touch typical of the dream-vision, the desert scene creates a sense of impending crisis. An abrupt heightening of style seems to adumbrate some change: in just over twenty lines there are two references to God and, in contrast to the rather bald recital of Aeneas's deeds after Carthage, a sudden wealth of concrete imagery. There is also a new spaciousness, striking after the enclosure of the Temple and its limited visual field; now the Narrator is able to look "As fer as that I myghte see" (483) and "as hye/ As kenne myghte I with myn ye" (498).

The crisis here is not only dramatic, deriving from the Narrator's frightening personal situation. It is also a narrative crisis reflecting the sterility of the episode of the Temple. The story of Dido and Aeneas stirred the Narrator's sympathy, but it has generated no further narrative material. Furthermore, it has shown that conflicting traditions exist, but has offered no way of reconciling them. The Narrator is at an impasse. There is no obvious next step; nothing has been or, it seems, will be explained.

In this anxious moment there is no appeal to love, reputation, or glory, topics which have usually been identified as the theme of the *House of Fame*. There is no suggestion that any of these can offer relief for the Narrator's distress. Instead the Narrator begs to be protected from "fantome and illusion." For us, "phantom" has rather a vague meaning: an apparition, a delusion of some sort, a haunting idea. It is not a common word in medieval literature. Its special status is indicated by the fact that in one early manuscript of the *House of Fame* it is underlined in red, along with classical references and exotic geographical names. But the word did, in the Middle Ages, possess several quite specific meanings. These would have alerted Chaucer's audience to possible dangers confronting the Narrator of the *House of Fame* as dreamer, as scholar, and as poet.

The word first appears in the Proem when the Narrator mentions four types of dream of whose causes he claims to be ignorant; they are "avisioun," "revelacioun," "fantome," and "oracle." Although the terminology of dreamlore is far from constant in medieval tradition, the generally accepted definition of "phantom" is found in Macrobius's commentary on Cicero's *Somnium Scipionis*.

> The apparition (*phantasma* or *visum*) comes upon one in the moment between wakefulness and slumber, in the so-called "first cloud of sleep." In this drowsy condition he thinks he is still fully awake and imagines he sees specters rushing at him or wandering vaguely about, differing from

natural creatures in size and shape. . . . To this class belongs the incubus. . . . The two types just described are of no assistance in foretelling the future; but by means of the other three [types of dream] we are gifted with the powers of divination.[1]

F. N. Robinson uses this definition in glossing "fantome" in the Narrator's prayer (493) as a kind of nightmare devoid of valid instruction: "The fantome . . . was often explained as produced by the operation of demons upon the mind of the sleeper, and the term illusioun was applied to their false revelations." As a dreamer, the Narrator of the *House of Fame* will certainly want to be protected against malign influence, and a landscape as desolate as the desert of Book I would give any dreamer reason to fear hallucination. But Chaucer's Narrator is no ordinary dreamer. He is a poet as well; indeed we are shortly to learn from the Eagle that a journey to Fame's palace is the Narrator's reward for "labour and devocion" in writing love poetry. To limit "phantom" to its pathological meaning is to ignore the moral and esthetic connotations that make the phenomenon especially dangerous for a dreamer who is also a poet.

Phantom—in Middle English *fantome*, in Old French *fantosme*, in Greek and Latin *phantasma*—denoted, in the Aristotelian theory of mental processes, an image which serves as intermediary between perception and understanding. It was a kind of "immaterial sensation" representing things already perceived or, by inference from these, things that could be perceived. It occurs in dreams and in waking life, but in both it is referrable to sensation or to waking experience. Without a phantom, no knowledge or thought can exist in the mind. The Aristotelian

1. *Macrobius' Commentary on the Dream of Scipio,* trans. William Stahl (New York, 1952), pp. 89–90. It is not certain that Chaucer drew his terminology from Macrobius alone, and C. S. Lewis, *The Discarded Image* (Cambridge, 1964), p. 54, suggests that Chaucer's classification may have been derived indirectly from Chalcidius's commentary on the *Timaeus* of Plato. But since Chalcidius does not speak of phantom, it is likely that Chaucer's knowledge of it does come from Macrobius.

definition of phantom was accepted by a number of medieval writers, particularly the scholastic philosophers who had been trained in the works of Aristotle. Thomas Aquinas writes, "Anima intellectiva non potest intellegere sine phantasmativus" (*Summa Contra Gentiles* 2, 80).

However, another definition of phantom was developed during the late classical period by the Stoics,[2] and although it was not generally used in scholastic treatises, it did persist in popular pseudoscientific literature, in encyclopedias, and in vernacular literature. Stoic psychologists developed the Aristotelian notion in support of an ethical system which emphasized the right use of reason. They therefore introduced a distinction between phantom and phantasy. Phantasy functions in the Stoic system as phantom does in the Aristotelian: it is a mental impression which reproduces reality and which serves as the basis for conceptual thought. Phantom, on the other hand, occurs only in dreams or waking illusions. Having no mimetic relation to reality, it conveys erroneous information to the intellect and is thus able to motivate irrational opinions or actions.

This separation of faculties was perpetuated by a number of medieval authorities. Augustine, for instance, distinguishes the imitative function of phantasy from the dangerously creative role of phantom.

> I imagine my father, whom I have often seen, in one way; my ancestor, whom I have never seen, in another. The first of these is phantasy, the second phantom. I find the former in memory, the latter in that motion of the soul which originates in what memory contains. . . . What I construct from what I have seen, I construct by memory; still, it is one thing to find a phantasy in the memory, and another to create a phantom from memory—all of

2. For the following discussion of "phantom" I am indebted to the exhaustive study of Prof. Murray Wright Bundy, *The Theory of Imagination in Classical and Mediaeval Thought* (Urbana, Ill., 1927).

which the power of the soul can do. But to accept phantom as knowledge is the gravest error.[3]

Augustine's example of the familiar father and the imagined ancestor reappears in the *Differentiarum* of Isidore, bishop of Seville. Isidore also retains Augustine's distinction between what is found in the mind and what is created there. He continues the definition as follows:

> Phantasy, then, is assembled by memory from perceived forms; phantom is created by the mind from unperceived forms. Now phantoms are created from nothing else than real forms abstracted from bodily sense; and, as they are received, it is quite easy to divide, multiply, contract, expand, arrange, or upset them—but if the truth be known, it is difficult to beware of and avoid them.[4]

As a psychological term, then, phantom denotes a mental process, or the product of a mental process, which is deceptive in that it does not accurately mirror the phenomenal world. Chaucer uses the word in this sense in the *Man of Law's Tale*. King Alla, assuming that his wife and child have died at sea by his mother's command, murders his mother in revenge and later travels to Rome to do penance for this deed. There he sees a child whose resemblance to Constance, his wife, is so striking that Alla begins to hope that this may be his lost son and that Constance too may be alive. The king struggles against his hope:

> "Parfay," thoghte he, "fantome is in myn heed!
> I oghte deme, of skilful juggement,
> That in the salte see my wyf is deed."
>
> *(B¹ 1037–39)*

Events prove Alla's surmise to be in fact no phantom, but his deliberate opposition between "fantome" and "skilful

3. Augustine, "De Musica," 6. 11. 32, in *Opera Omnia* (Paris,1841), vol. 1. Cited in Bundy, *Imagination*, p. 161, n. 43.
4. Isidore, *Differentiarum*, 1: 216 (*PL* 83: 32), "Inter *Phantasiam* et *phantasma*."

juggement" endows the former with distinctly psychological significance.

It is not difficult to perceive the logic whereby the scientific term was externalized to designate visual rather than conceptual appearances, the object perceived rather than a stage in the act of perception. By this extension of meaning, phantom came to include various kinds of illusory phenomena. The illusion may be associated with the mythical substructure of romance, as when the Green Knight rides into Arthur's court on New Year's Day and astonishes the entire assembly:

For fele sellyes had thay sen, bot such never are,
For-thi for fantoum & fayryghe the folk there hit demed.
(*Sir Gawain and the Green Knight*, 1, 239–40)

Or the event may be a divine miracle, either Christian or pagan, which is mistaken by observers for sleight of hand or diabolical interference. Thus in the *Roman de la Rose* Pygmalion addresses his statue which Venus has transformed into a living woman:

"Dou vient donques cete merveille?
Est ce fantosme ou anemis
Qui s'est en mon image mis?"
(*21149–51*)

A Wycliffite translation of the New Testament relates the disciples' reaction to Jesus walking on the water as follows:

But in the fourthe wakyng of the night, he cam to hem walkynge above the see. and thei, seynge hym walking on the see, weren disturblid, and seiden, That it is a fantum, and for drede thei crieden.[5]

5. *The New Testament in English*, ed. J. Forshall and F. Madden (Oxford, 1879); the locus is Matt. 14: 26. "Phantom" is also used at Mark 6: 49, where the same incident is related. The Greek Bible and the Vulgate use *phantasma* in these places. The King James version has "spirit," and most modern Bibles use "spirit," "ghost," or "apparition." However these words lack the ominous overtones of "phantom," which distinguish the false vision from the genuine spiritual confrontation.

Of course no genuine miracle can be considered a phantom in any sense. As Augustine put it, "Si phantasma fuit corpus Christi, fefellit Christus: Et si fallit, veritas non est; est autem veritas Christus, non igitur phantasma fuit corpus eius."[6]

Once associated with deceptive objects, phantom may be applied to moral as well as to visual illusions. This usage is found, as might be expected, primarily in such didactic texts as the *Ancren Riwle*:

> Al Holi Writ is ful of warnings of eie. David seide, "Averte oculos meos ne videant vanitatem." Loverd, seith David, wend awei mine eien vrom the worldes dweole & hir fantesme.[7]

The late thirteenth-century "omnibus poem" *Cursor Mundi*, in deploring those people who devote time to worldly vanities, remarks:

> Hit is but fantom for to say
> To day hit is to morwe away.[8]

And, in the Wycliffite tract entitled "Three Things Destroy This World," it is claimed that by the display of worldly goods in markets, "lordis & othere men ben drawen fro thinkynge of god & hevenely thingis, & setten here wittis & likynges in thes newe vanytees & fantom of worldly glorie."[9]

Most of the examples I have cited so far, which use "phantom" to designate an erroneous idea or appearance, reflect the passivity implicit in medieval psychology. Systems of faculty psychology assigned each mental power to its proper area in the brain, and the personality as a whole

---

6. Augustine, *Lib. 83 Quaest.*, q. 13.
7. *The Ancren Riwle*, ed. James Morton (London, 1853), p. 62. This is from part 2, section 1, "Of sight."
8. *Cursor Mundi*, lines 55–56, in EETS, vol. 57/1, ed. Rev. Richard Morris (London, 1874).
9. *The English Works of Wyclif*, EETS, vol. 74, ed. F. D. Matthew (London, 1880). According to the editor, there is no certainty of date or authorship for this tract.

was thought to be subject to one or another of its own aspects, whether intellect, imagination, or passion. Because of its origin as a psychological term, phantom is seen as something which imposes itself on the mind, leading it to misinterpret reality. In some medieval usage, though, another shift in meaning occurs, so that phantom acquires an active sense. It becomes a synonym for fraud or a euphemism for lie; thus it is something that can be voluntarily performed or avoided. Indeed the French made verbs of it: *fantosmer*, to deceive, and *enfantosmer*, to enchant by magic. The heroine of the Old French chante-fable *Aucassin et Nicolette* is accused of phantom (deceit) when she asks a shepherd to relay the message to Aucassin that there is an unusually valuable beast in the forest which he must pursue. "Je le dirai?" answers the shepherd, either taking the courtly code *au pied de la lettre* or understanding it all too well:

> Dehait ait qui ja en parlera, ne qui ja le dira! C'est fantosmes que vos dites, qu'il n'a si ciere beste en ceste forest . . . dont uns des menbres vaille plus de dex deniers u de trois au plus, et vos parlés de si grant avoir!
>
> *(Prose 18)*

In this sense the word is also found in Wace's *Roman de Rou*. Louis d'Outremer, trying to camouflage his planned abduction of the Norman Duke Richard, tells the Normans that he will take the young Duke to his own court at Laon to learn courtesy with his own son. The ploy is successful: "Tant lor a dist fantosmes, ke déchéuz les a."[10]

Finally, phantom comes to be associated with literary illusion. Partly because of its alliterative value it is often paired with "fable"—a word which in its strict sense meant a fictional invention, but which in popular usage had become a synonym for falsehood. We read in *Cursor Mundi*:

10. Robert Wace, *Le Roman de Rou*, ed. Frederic Pluquet (Rouen, 1827), line 2914.

What bote is hite of right to rede
That never founden is in dede
Much to here & litil to holde
But were a ribaudry us tolde
Of a fantom or a fabul
That wolde we holde in herte stable.

(23857–62)

Perhaps the most distinguished "fables" to be described as phantasmic are the writings of Dante. Fra Guido Vernani, attacking Dante's political treatise *De Monarchia*, wrote, not long after the poet's death, of "certain beautiful vessels filled with poison and belonging to the devil." Among such vessels, Vernani noted, was a certain one—and a marginal manuscript note reads, "loquitur de dante florentino"—

> sophistically prolix and full of fantastical poetizing and exotic words, pleasing in eloquence—who, by his poetical phantoms and figments . . . fraudulently led, with his sweet siren songs, not only infirm but even learned souls to the loss of salvation-bearing truth.[11]

These two examples suggest what must have been for Chaucer—indeed what would be for any poet—the most powerful meaning of phantom: the deception of the written word. The artist may be victim of delusive images conveyed in an all-inclusive literary tradition; like other men he may suffer from phantoms. Unlike other men, though, the artist can also impose delusive images on others, for if his imaginative vision is faulty he may create a phantasmic work—a useless or misleading work whose fiction is not "true" by any imaginable standard.

Phantom, then, means far more than a bad dream or a pathological condition associated with sleep. Having noted

---

11. Vernani, *De Reprobatione Monarchiae*, ed. Nevio Matteini, in *Il Piu' Antico Oppositore Politico di Dante* (Padua, 1958). As Boccaccio notes in his life of Dante, *De Monarchia* was condemned by the ecclesiastical establishment because it had been used by Ludwig of Bavaria to support his struggle against Pope John XXII.

some of its perceptual, moral, and esthetic meanings, we may return to the Narrator's prayer at the end of Book I and read that prayer as a kind of invocation. It is an invocation addressed to Christ rather than to the classical deities of the three conventional invocations which open the three narrative sections of the *House of Fame*. Unlike the others, it asks not merely for literary competence but for the right use of imagination. That is the heart of the crisis which the Narrator experiences on leaving the Temple of Venus, for in the Temple he had encountered the problem of imaginative truth in its most immediate form: the conflict of values within the medieval literary tradition. It is the purpose of the concluding prayer to expand our terms of reference beyond the troublesome dialectic of conflicting literary traditions, just as in the Proem the opening and closing wish—"God turn every dream to good"—allows us to transcend a futile debate about dream-lore.

With unconscious irony, the nineteenth-century literary historian Hippolyte Taine once described the *House of Fame* as a "phantasmagoria"—an assembly of phantoms or insubstantial images. Taine meant that the work had no serious moral or intellectual purpose, no coherent structure, nor much esthetic interest beyond the exotic: "a glow of colors and a jumble of forms." Taine's view is based on a misunderstanding of late medieval form and style: he deprecates the Gothic cathedral along with Chaucer's works, and for the same reasons. Unjust as Taine's critique may be, his epithet does suggest the sense of unresolved conflict that characterizes the *House of Fame*, and the absence from that work of a fixed narrative point of view. That lack is both the thematic center of the poem and, for many readers, its main esthetic flaw. Its source is the poet's perception that tradition, or fame, offers no certain truth: he is reluctant to commit himself to a traditional role or to any single traditional point of view. *Troilus and Criseyde* poses a similar difficulty, but there it is successfully resolved; the reader can commit himself to the characters and to the love story, if not to a literary tradition. In the *House of Fame*, tradition is treated so ironically from the start that we cannot commit ourselves to it; and nothing else—neither character nor plot—is sufficiently developed to win our commitment. Without that, the poem remains an intellectual exercise, though an extremely interesting exercise and an important one in the development of Chaucer's art.

7
The Limits of Science

s if in answer to the Narrator's prayer at the end of
Book I, a great golden eagle swoops down from the
sky and seizes "Geffrey," rescuing him from the desert that
lies outside the Temple of Venus. So frightened and aston-
ished is Geffrey that he faints, and on recovering he is
treated in mid-air to a series of lectures. As a figure with an
illustrious traditional background, the garrulous bird is
well qualified to convey important information: his literary
antecedents are found in the Greek myth of Ganymede, in
the Bible, in patristic biblical commentary, and in Dante's
Divine Comedy.[1] He provides a motive for the dramatic
action of the second and third books of the poem, revealing
that Jupiter, having observed Geffrey's conscientious labor

> To make bookys, songes, dytees,
> In ryme, or elles in cadence,
> As thou best canst, in reverence
> Of Love, and of hys servantes eke,
> *(622–25)*

has decided to reward the poet with a journey to the House
of Fame, where he will be able to observe more closely the
doings of "Loves folk." The Eagle also sketches an amusing
portrait of Geffrey at home, who, like Chaucer himself,
must divide his time between business and books:

1. See, for example, Exodus 19:24, Job 39:27, Jeremiah 48:40, 49:22,
Ezekiel 17:3. In Dante, Purgatory 9: 13–33; Paradise 18: 106–8; 19; 20.

For when thy labour doon al ys,
And hast mad alle thy rekenynges,
In stede of reste and newe thynges,
Thou goost hom to thy hous anoon;
And, also domb as any stoon,
Thou sittest at another book
Tyl fully daswed ys thy look,
And lyvest thus as an heremyte,
Although thyn abstynence ys lyte.

(652–60)

At Fame's palace, the Eagle says, Geffrey will hear "Both sothe sawes and lesynges," for news of everything that is said and done on earth comes to that place. Geffrey responds that he can hardly believe such a thing, and the Eagle's contentious proof of his assertion occupies the next 150 lines, or about one-quarter of the entire book. A versatile rhetorician, he uses several techniques of persuasion. The argument opens with a brief description of Fame's dwelling-place imitated from Ovid's *Metamorphoses* (12, 43–52).

Hir paleys stant, as I shal seye,
Ryght even in myddes of the weye
Betwixen hevene, erthe, and see;
That what so ever in al these three
Is spoken, either privy or apert,
The way therto ys so overt,
And stant eke in so juste a place
That every soun mot to hyt pace,
Or what so cometh from any tonge,
Be hyt rouned, red, or songe,
Or spoke in suerte or drede,
Certeyn, hyt moste thider nede.

(713–24)

After this introductory description drawn from literary authority, the argument progresses to theoretical discussion based on logical and empirical proof:

Now herkene wel, for-why I wille
Tellen the a propre skille
And a worthy demonstracion . . . .
(725–27)

The "propre skille" ("correct argument") is an exposition
of the scientific principle of natural place (729–81), while
the demonstration illustrates that principle with an analogy to empirical observation (793–822). By way of conclusion the Eagle summarizes his arguments (823–52) and
congratulates himself on having presented such a convincing proof of the nature of Geffrey's destination (853–63).

Scientific theory, then, and the empirical illustration of
that theory form the body of the Eagle's monologue. At the
center of that monologue is a theory of natural causation
and, implicitly, a particular attitude toward nature. According to the Eagle, the operation of fame is governed by
natural laws and demonstrates the working of those laws.
The importance of nature to the Eagle's argument is suggested by the appearance of the word "kynde" and its
variants four times in the first twenty lines of the passage
and eight times in its last thirty lines. Stones fall, smoke
rises, rivers flow, and sound comes to Fame's palace by
virtue of "kyndely enclynyng," or the natural tendency of
each element to seek its proper place:

> loo, thou maist alday se
> That any thing that hevy be,
> As stoon, or led, or thyng of wighte,
> And bere hyt never so hye on highte,
> Lat goo thyn hand, hit falleth doun.
> Ryght so seye I be fyr or soun,
> Or smoke, or other thynges lyghte,
> Alwey they seek upward on highte.
> While ech of hem is at his large,
> Lyght thing upward, and dounward charge.
> And for this cause mayst thou see

That every ryver to the see
Enclyned ys to goo by kynde . . . .

(737–49)

This doctrine the Eagle correctly ascribes to "Aristotle and daun Platon,/ And other clerkes many oon" (759–60), for in different forms it appears first in Plato and then in Aristotle, and for centuries was the basis of medieval natural philosophy. The axiom that like moves toward like is, in the *Timaeus,* "an ultimate unexplained assumption"[2] following from the theory that the phenomenal world is a copy whose elements tend to seek the eternal model. Plato invokes the principle of like to like as the cause of order in chaos (*Timaeus,* 53a), of vision (45b–c), and of digestion (81d). Chaucer would have encountered the idea in a number of well-known texts, among them the works of Boethius and the twelfth-century neo-Platonists of Chartres, the *Roman de la Rose,* the *Ovide Moralisé,* and Dante's *Divine Comedy.*

For late medieval philosophers, though, it was Aristotle who definitively stated the theory of natural place. It appears in several of the scientific works—particularly the *Physics* and the *De Caelo*—that were translated from Greek and Arabic during the twelfth and thirteenth centuries. The premise of Aristotle's theory of natural place is not the existence of a world of archetypal forms, which mundane elements strive to reach or imitate. It proceeds rather from his definition of nature. The "nature" of a thing Aristotle defines as its capacity for movement, and it is that potential for movement of various sorts that distinguishes natural objects from artificial ones.

Some things exist by nature, some from other causes. Animals and their bodily organs, plants, and the physical elements—earth, air, fire, water—

2. Professor Cornford's phrase in his edition of the *Timaeus, Plato's Cosmology* (London, 1937), p. 169. The *Timaeus,* in the fourth-century translation and commentary of Chalcidius, was one of the few Platonic treatises known to the Middle Ages.

such things as these we say exist "by nature." There is one particular in which all the objects just named are observed to differ from things that are not constituted by nature: each of them has within itself a principle of movement and rest—whether this movement be locomotion, or growth and decrease, or qualitative change.[3]

Among objects to which motion is essential, a further distinction is made between motion generated from within the object (as with plants or animals) and motion that is natural but derived from an external source (the motion of fire and other elements). The motion of inorganic substances Aristotle explains as follows:

> We must now seek the reason for the motion of light and heavy objects into their respective positions. The reason is that they each have a natural tendency in some direction or other, and that this tendency constitutes the essence of lightness and heaviness, the former consisting in an upward, the latter in a downward tendency.[4]

The Eagle's exposition of natural place is well within the orthodox tradition. Since air is a light substance, its nature is to rise; since sound is nothing but broken air, its natural tendency will be to rise until it arrives at Fame's palace. But the Eagle is not satisfied to rely on logic alone. He demonstrates the transmission of sound through air "be experience," using the analogy of water into which a stone is thrown:[5]

3. *Physics* 2: 1. From the translation by Philip Wheelwright (New York, 1935).
4. Ibid., 8: 4.
5. The image of a stone thrown into water is fairly well known in medieval scientific and encyclopedic literature. It appears in Boethius (*De Musica* 1: 14) and in Vincent of Beauvais (*Speculum Naturale* 5: 18), in their expositions of the nature of sound. Other writers used it for other purposes. Averroes, commenting on Aristotle's *Physics*, cites it to illustrate Aristotle's theory of projectile motion, according to which the medium (air or water) continues to transmit motion to the object after the original mover has lost contact with the object (in *Aris-*

Wel wost thou, hyt wol make anoon
A litel roundell as a sercle,
Paraunter broad as a covercle;
And ryght anoon thow shal see wel,
That whel wol cause another whel
And that the thridde, and so forth, brother,
Every sercle causynge other
Wydder than hymselve was; . . .
Ryght so of ayr, my leve brother;
Everych ayr another stereth
More and more, and speche up bereth,
Or voys, or noys, or word, or soun,
Ay through multiplicacioun,
Til hyt be atte Hous of Fame—
Take hyt in ernest or in game.

(790–822)

In fact we have to take the entire lecture in earnest *and* in game, for however respectable the Eagle's scientific theory, however impressive his literary pedigree, he remains a comic character. Part of his comic effect comes from characterization: his brash, colloquial manner of speech, and the patronizing pomposity with which he instructs the timorous Geffrey. Another source of humor in the Eagle's monologue is that its elaborate rhetoric cannot disguise an unconvincing argument. It is not science but a parody of science: the exaggeration into absurdity of methodological

---

totelis *Opera cum Averrois Commentariis*, 4: 430 verso, col. 1; reprinted [Frankfurt, 1962] in facsimile from Venice edition of 1562). Refuting the Aristotelian theory of projectile motion, Jean Buridan cites the same example to support his own theory of impetus (*Quaestiones octavi libri physicorum*, cited in Pierre Duhem, *Etudes sur Léonard de Vinci* [Paris, 1886] 3: 39.

An interesting theological use of the image appears in the Sentence Commentary of Franciscus de Marchi (c. 1320). Attempting to prove that God can work directly and without intermediate causes, the author turns to projectile motion as an example of immediate effect. In order to use this example, however, he must first disprove Aristotle's notion that the medium transmits motion and is thus a cause of motion. The commentary is excerpted in Anneliese Maier, *Die Impetustheorie der Scholastik* (Vienna, 1940), p. 52.

tendencies already inherent in scholastic science. Even in Aristotle's version, the theory of natural place is nearly tautological: elements and creatures behave as they do because it is their nature to do so. The Eagle's analogy to disturbed water was fairly widely used in the scientific and encyclopedic literature on sound, but analogy alone is not proof. From beginning to end, the Eagle's speech relies on tautology, analogy, non sequitur, reductive simplicity, abuse of the syllogism, circular argument, and "proofs" that prove nothing. To clinch his dubious argument, the Eagle challenges anyone who disagrees with it to prove the contrary—a very different task from proving only that the argument is inadequate. Indeed, to prove the contrary of any cosmological theory would be virtually impossible given the lack of empirical evidence. Certainly Geffrey is not one to think of contradicting his mentor, but his reply to the Eagle's eager request for an opinion is noticeably reserved:

> "A good persuasion,"
> Quod I, "hyt is; and lyk to be
> Ryght so as thou hast preved me."

In focusing on "persuasion," or formal argument itself, this comment seems tactfully to avoid the question of truth. Geffrey also omits any clear statement of personal response to the lecture, noting only that reality may well resemble the Eagle's version of it—a distinct deprecation of the weight of his "proofs."

In the Eagle's monologue, then, we can observe a dialectic similar to that in the Proem and in Book i. In all three sections the subject matter is traditional enough—dream lore, the story of Dido and Aeneas, scientific theory. In all three, Chaucer's treatment of his material seriously qualifies its traditional authority. Although by Chaucer's time the work of Ockham, Buridan, and others had already stripped Aristotelian science of much of its earlier prestige, it is doubtful that Chaucer knew contemporary natural philosophy well enough to found an ironic critique of

Aristotle upon it. His other references to Aristotle suggest that Chaucer had a superficial and probably indirect knowledge of the Philosopher, together with substantial respect for his authority. To what end, then, does he parody Aristotelian method, and reduce Jove's messenger to a cracker-barrel sage?

It will be easier to understand the burlesque of scientific method if we approach it not as an isolated stylistic phenomenon, but as part of the structural dialectic of Book 2. The monologue represents an empirical view of the world which, like the Narrator's Ovidian sentimentality in Book 1, appears in the poem expressly to be undercut. That purpose is accomplished in two ways: by the humorous treatment of scientific material in the Eagle's monologue and by the juxtaposition of an alternate world view in the mythical material which follows the monologue. It is this process of cumulative critique, together with its resolution, that forms the thematic center of Book 2.

The Eagle displays a naive confidence in the trappings of logic and in an oversimplified view of natural causation. Clearly, he assumes that the real causes of things can in fact be discovered by observation and reason, that the universe is really accessible to the operations of sense and intellect. It was just such willingness to rely on human faculties alone in the search for truth that critics of classical logic had considered the most dangerous aspect of that discipline. Even when presented in a far more persuasive and sophisticated manner than Chaucer's Eagle is capable of, the Aristotelian world view eliminates the sense of mystery common to both Platonism and Christianity. "To purge the philosophical consciousness of its mythical and metaphorical elements"[6] was Aristotle's aim, but the foundation of Christian cosmology is myth itself. *Credo ut intelligam* was one phrase—St. Anselm's—summarizing the Christian idea of the relation of knowledge to belief; *fides quarens intellectum* was another. Whether Aristotle

6. Werner Jaeger, *Aristotle* (Oxford, 1923), p. 377.

succeeded in eliminating all myth and metaphor from his philosophical system it is not my purpose to determine; moreover it is difficult to locate a "pure" Aristotelianism in the Middle Ages, since the original material had been overlaid with accretions from neo-Platonic, Arabic, Jewish, and Christian translators and commentators. Nevertheless the structure of the Aristotelian universe was as evident to medieval scholars as were its differences from the Christian universe. It is a series of causes and effects governed throughout by laws that can be observed in nature, deduced from natural principles and predicted. These laws determine the behavior of even the highest term in the series, the unmoved mover.

Such a system has no room for several features of the Christian world view: the creation of nature ex nihilo, the existence of a single omnipotent deity whose will is the prime cause of all things, and the consequent contingency that is demonstrated when God intervenes in nature to perform one of the miracles that only faith can accept. The difference between the two cosmologies is clearly stated by Galen (130–200), the Greek physician and writer, many of whose treatises were known to medieval scholars.

> If God wished to make a stone instantly into a man, it would not be in his power. And it is here that our doctrine, and that of Plato and of all the Greeks who have correctly undertaken the treatment of nature, differs from that of Moses. For Moses, it suffices that God willed that matter be given a form, and thereupon it received that form. He considers that all things are possible to God, even if He wishes to make ashes into a horse or an ox. We do not think that way, but say that some things are impossible by nature, but these God does not even attempt.[7]

Besides its outright contradiction of Christian doctrine, a rational-empirical philosophy must have eliminated the

7. Cited in translation in Joseph Owens, *The Doctrine of Being in the Aristotelian Metaphysics* (Toronto, 1951), p. 305.

fear of cosmos that constitutes the emotional ground for myth. It is easier, for instance—or safer—to imagine a magical creative moment than to contemplate the terrifying prospect of a world without beginning or end. To subordinate the self to eternity requires rigorous repression of the primitive desire for special protection against the void or for special favor within it. Fear of cosmos generates the notion of intellectual limits, something alien to Aristotle. "All men by nature desire to know" are the opening words of the *Metaphysics,* and succeeding chapters develop the ideas that conceptual knowledge is the best, that universal principles are knowable, that conceptual knowledge is valuable for its own sake. But for those who, unlike Socrates, cannot feel "at ease in Zion," that desire to know is mere vain curiosity. For them natural place is not simply an analytic concept but a moral imperative: like the stars and the elements, man ought not to aspire beyond his "natural place." He may be tempted to go where he does not belong, to know more than he can understand, to wield a power he cannot control: but failure is certain.

This view of things Aristotle explicitly rejects:

> Indeed, if there were any truth in the poet's view that divinity naturally tends to be jealous, the jealousy would doubtless manifest itself in this direction especially, which would mean that those who excel in the pursuit of wisdom are less fortunate than other men. Divinity, however, cannot be jealous: and, as the proverb says, "Bards tell many a lie." And let us not esteem any other knowledge higher than this, for the most divine knowledge is always the most estimable.
>
> *(Metaphysics I.2)*

The Christian God, like Jahweh before him, is nothing if not jealous; the mythic Judaeo-Christian universe is dangerous, mysterious, and impervious to men's efforts to understand it. To the Christian, perfection (God) is infinite; what is imperfect (the created universe) is limited; so that the world cannot be eternal, nor can man hope to understand God. For Aristotle, however, perfection is finite; so that the first principle is comprehensible to men. Order in the Aristotelian universe makes that universe accessible to reason; order in the Christian universe makes it inaccessible, for the rational faculty is subsumed within that order and limited by it.

Naturally Chaucer's Eagle does not allude to the possibility of a transcendental or mythic critique of his scientific material, nor does he mention the temptation to overvalue a purely rationalistic cosmology. Nonethless such a perspective is not absent from Book 2. It is stated indirectly, through exemplary references and anecdotes and through symbolic actions that follow the Eagle's monologue.

After his extended argument, the Eagle with his passenger reaches such a height "That al the world . . . / No more semed than a prikke" (906–7). This vantage point only a few others had attained before Geffrey. The Eagle mentions four of the aerial travellers best known to medieval readers, noting that Geffrey has now surpassed even these:

> . . . half so high as this
> Nas Alixandre Macedo;
> Ne the kyng, Daun Scipio,
> That saw in drem, at poynt devys,
> Helle and erthe and paradys:
> Ne eke the wrechche Dedalus,
> Ne his child, the nyce Ykarus,
> That fleigh so highe that the hete
> Hys wynges malt, and he fel wete
> In myd the see, and ther he dreynte,
> For whom was maked much compleynte.
>   (914–24)

More than analogies based on the shared experience of flight and a celestial point of view, more than standards by which to gauge Geffrey's incredible height, these references operate in context as brief exempla. The four figures named were commonly used in medieval tradition to point a particular moral: that men must acknowledge limits to their understanding of nature and, consequently, to their power over it.

The most fully developed of these references is the last, to Dedalus and his son Icarus. Chaucer outlines the story, whose moral—that man ought not to aspire beyond his natural role—is strongly implied even in Ovid's version of the myth (*Met.* 8). In later versions the lesson was made explicit. Chaucer knew the early fourteenth-century French allegorization of the *Metamorphoses*, the *Ovide Moralisé*. This text interprets the flight in two ways. First, the man who flies too high is the one who deceives himself through pride, supposing that the goods of life proceed from himself alone and not from divine grace (8. 1841–49). Second, those who aspire to the height of knowledge ("la hautesce de savoir") will be thrown down to perdition, since their learning is not directed to the knowledge of God (8. 1891–1903).

The second aerial traveller the Eagle mentions is Scipio. Human limitation is the theme of *Scipio's Dream*, which, originally part of Cicero's *De Republica*, was known to Chaucer in the commentary of Macrobius. The narrator, Scipio Africanus the Younger, tells of a dream in which his ancestor, Scipio the Elder, escorts him to the empyrean sphere. From this point he sees the earth so small that he learns the relative insignificance of his empire (chapter 3). The moral is repeated when Africanus describes men's inability to hear the harmony of the spheres (chapter 5), when he shows the futility of striving after fame (chapter 7), and when he reproaches his descendant for contemplating suicide in order to achieve immediate immortality. "Men were created," he says, "with the understanding that they were to look after that sphere called earth" (chapter 3). Resignation, then, to the limits of our nature, and renunciation of ultimate knowledge or power, are the lessons of *Scipio's Dream.*

The episode of Alexander's cosmic flight appears in several texts of the protean and immensely popular Alexander legend. It seems to have seized the medieval imagination more than other motifs in the story, for numerous graphic representations show Alexander in the gryphon-drawn cart in which his ascent was made. Although lessons in humility are abundant in most texts, the ascent itself is not usually moralized. Chaucer may have known a moralized version of the flight, or he may simply have transferred exemplary meaning to it on the basis of other moralized episodes. Whether or not Chaucer had a specific source, the figure of Alexander had become by Chaucer's time an example of the overreaching worldly ambition that requires and receives some check. The *Speculum Historiale,* part of Vincent of Beauvais' monumental encyclopedia *Speculum Majus* (thirteenth century), tells the story of Alexander at some length in Book 4. Some chapter headings must suffice here to indicate Vincent's use of the material: 31, *de luxuria Alexandri, et superbia; 42, de insolentia Alexandri post victoriam; 61, de iactantia et ambitione Alexandri; 62, de superstitione eiusdem, ac livore.*

Surprisingly harsh is Boccaccio's judgment of Alexander, considering that his stated aim in the *Genealogia* is simply to collect information. According to some versions of the legend, Alexander was the son of Jove who, in the form of a snake, lay with Olympia, Alexander's mother. Why, then, does Boccaccio exclude Alexander from the sons of Jove listed in his *Genealogia?* Taking up that question, Boccaccio interprets this feature of the legend as Alexander's own political propaganda, an attempt to cultivate worship of himself.

> O foolish desire of a famous youth, to choose to have been born from adultery rather than from marriage; to choose to have your mother unchaste rather than chaste; to choose to be the son of a

serpent rather than of Philip the most excellent
king; and to judge what is spurious to be better
than what is legitimate.

(Liber 13, cap. 71)

Not only foolish but hateful is such deliberate deception,
Boccaccio concludes, and so, because of his ambitious character, Alexander is deservedly rejected.

Since the Eagle's references to Alexander, Scipio, Dedalus, and Icarus are not interpreted in the text of the poem,
their symbolic impact depends on the reader's knowledge
of how they were used in medieval literature and scholarship. Yet Chaucer does not leave his point submerged. He
makes it unavoidably clear in the story of Phaeton, which
the Eagle proceeds to tell as an etiological explanation of the
Milky Way, now conveniently in sight. Through this extended mythical exemplum the Eagle can repeat directly
the moral that has remained implicit until now. He can also
provide a comment on his own scientific lecture. Geffrey
shares with Phaeton, as with the other mythical and legendary figures already mentioned, not only an airborne
adventure but the possibility of abusing his position. Be-
lieving himself capable of controlling the chariot of his
father Phoebus (the sun), Phaeton overestimates both his
skill and his proper role. The consequence of this self-decep-
tion is disaster to the world and to Phaeton himself.

> The carte-hors gonne wel espye
> That he koude no governaunce,
> And gonne for to lepe and launce,
> And beren hym now up, now doun . . .
>   and they anoon
> Gonne up to mounte and doun descende,
> Til bothe the eyr and erthe brende;
> Til Jupiter, loo, atte laste,
> Hym slow, and fro the carte caste.

> *(944–56)*

Like Phaeton, Geffrey finds himself in an exalted position:
he has begun to learn some of the laws of nature and has

seen beneath him the world and its creatures. Lest Geffrey delude himself as to his own relation to this plenitude, the Eagle provides a good-natured warning in the *moralitas* with which he ends the story of Phaeton:

> "Loo, ys it not a gret myschaunce
> To lete a fool han govcrnaunce
> Of thing that he can not demeyne?"
>
> *(957–59)*

In the structure of Book 2 so far, classical myth operates as a kind of reprimand to classical science. The Eagle's optimistic faith in intellect and observation as the keys to nature is balanced by the mythic perception of a mysterious universe. The abstract and somewhat mechanical series of natural causes is opposed to the community of anthropomorphic gods with power to punish and reward. There seems to be as little basis for choice between these alternate cosmologies as there was for choice between Virgil and Ovid in Book 1. In fact Geffrey does not explicitly choose between them—not, at least, in terms the Eagle has laid down. Still, he does find a way out of the dilemma, as he has done twice before.

With his concluding *moralitas* about Phaeton, the Eagle suddenly soars even higher. Until now, Geffrey has been rather passive, but at this point his behavior changes: he forgets his earlier fear and recovers his power of speech, which so far has consisted largely of monosyllabic replies. Geffrey's first spontaneous words are a short prayer in praise of God, the creator and cause of all he sees:

> "O God!" quod I, "that made Adam,
> Moche ys thy myght and thy noblesse!"
>
> *(970–71)*

As in earlier sections of the poem, Geffrey now resorts to Christian doctrine as a way of transcending choice. That transcendence—an intellectual breakthrough—Geffrey represents in a figure borrowed from Boethius's *De Consolatione Philosophiae* (4, metrum 1), which Chaucer probably had already begun to translate. His paraphrase provides an interpretation of the symbolic eagle-borne journey:

> "A thought may flee so hye,
> Wyth fetheres of Philosophye,
> To passen everych element;
> And whan he hath so fer ywent,
> Than may be seen, behynde hys bak,
> Cloude,"—and al that y of spak.
>
> *(973–78)*

In its Boethian context this image belongs to a short allegory of the mind's ascent to the last heaven and beyond, where it becomes God's knight; that is, it achieves true knowledge of God. Chaucer would have learned from Boethius, then, that flight may represent not merely an intellectual adventure but one whose goal is religious truth. Despite its lack of what Matthew Arnold was to call "high seriousness," Geffrey's journey does attain religious truth of a kind: a qualified and perhaps, to the orthodox, an unsatisfactory kind, but a truth which permits Geffrey to transcend conflict through faith.

That process is repeated once again in Geffrey's renunciation of any attempt fully to understand the terms of his existence. Echoing the words of St. Paul (2 Cor. 12:2) he says,

> Thoo gan y waxen in a were,
> And seyde, "I wot wel y am here;
> But wher in body or in gost
> I not, ywys; but God, thou wost!"
> For more clere entendement
> Nas me never yit ysent.
>
> *(979–84)*

Paradoxically, the clear understanding ("entendement") which Geffrey achieves here is due to his acceptance of doubt ("were"), and to the fideistic transcendence of doubt expressed here and in his earlier spontaneous prayer. These last few lines offer a miniature model of the fideistic process. Subjective experience ("I know that I am here") provides no absolute certainty ("But whether in body or spirit I do not know"); therefore one relies on faith for another kind of certainty ("But God, you know"). The revelation is not merely that rational choice is impossible, but that it is unnecessary.

The "leap of faith" confers a certain freedom on Geffrey. No longer confined within the narrow limits of what can be proved, he can accept a broader definition of truth than logical or empirical truth. Having professed his faith, he is free to believe whatever does not directly contradict Christian doctrine. He can therefore assent to the poetic cosmologies that he has found in such medieval classics as Martianus Capella's *De Nuptiis Philologiae et Mercurii* and Alanus's *Anticlaudianus* (985–90). A few lines later the Eagle invites Geffrey to observe for himself the exact positions of the stars. The offer is made to Geffrey in his capacity as a lover of poetry, that he may add personal experience to his theoretical knowledge of classical mythic astrology. But the limits of science and of experience have already been defined, so that poetic cosmology needs no empirical corroboration. Accordingly, Geffrey declines the offer: he is too old, he is willing to trust the poetic authorities, the light of the stars would probably ruin his eyes in any case (991–1017).

"That may wel be," replies the Eagle, with untypical brevity, to Geffrey's confession of natural limitation, and soon thereafter they reach their destination. The Eagle guarantees Geffrey that no harm will come to him at Fame's palace, but this sanguine confidence is not shared. One guesses that Geffrey, like the narrator of the *Parliament of Fowls,* enters the otherworldly place with a helpful shove from his guide:

> Y nyste how, but in a strete
> He sette me fair on my fete,
> And seyde, "Walke forth a pas,

> And take thyn aventure or cas,
> That thou shalt fynde in Fames place."
>
> *(1049–53)*

Yet it is not finally his own authority the Eagle invokes in order to reassure Geffrey, for the second book closes, like the first, with a brief prayer on Geffrey's behalf:

> "And God of heven sende the grace
> Some good to lernen in this place."

In Book 1, Morpheus had been invoked as guardian of dreams, but Christ protects from phantom and illusion. In Book 2, Jove is said to initiate the dramatic action, but God's grace is requested for whatever enlightenment may occur at Fame's palace. The progression in both books from invocation to prayer—from classical to Christian deity, from public to private mode of address—parallels the movement that has been expressed in the structure of each division of the poem so far: a movement from traditions that are relative, feigned, or flawed to a truth which is absolute, eternal, and perfect.

8

History and Story

The climax of Geffrey's journey to Fame's court appears to be the judgment scene in which the "variant goddess" distributes good reputation, bad reputation,
and anonymity to nine groups of petitioners. The scene
demonstrates some possible permutations of desire, merit,
and reward. The first three groups deserve good fame and
request it. But the allotment of reputation is random and,
to Geffrey, incomprehensible:

> And somme of hem she graunted sone,
> And somme she werned wel and faire,
> And somme she graunted the contraire
> Of her axyng outterly.
> But thus I seye yow, trewely,
> What her cause was, y nyste.
> For of this folk ful wel y wiste,
> They hadde good fame ech deserved
> Although they were dyversely served;
> Ryght as her suster, dame Fortune,
> Ys wont to serven in comune.
>
> *(1538–48)*

The fourth and fifth companies have done good works but,
having acted only "for Goddys love," wish to be forgotten.
That wish is granted the former group and denied the latter. Although the sixth and seventh companies fully deserve anonymity, their members having lived idly all their
lives and done "neither that nor this," both ask for good

87

fame. This is granted to the members of one group but denied to those in the other, who are indignantly berated for their indifference. The eighth set of petitioners request a good name despite their admission of "the grettest wikkidnesse/ That any herte kouthe gesse." Fame denies their request, for

> "Al be ther in me no justice,
> Me lyste not to doo hyt now,
> Ne this nyl I not graunte yow."
> *(1820–22)*

Only in the ninth and last company is there a just correlation between desire, merit, and reward: those in this group have delighted in evil, ask to be remembered as they were, and are granted ill fame. That Chaucer does not, however, show outright wickedness achieving good fame is perhaps a vestige of his will to believe in some form of absolute justice.

This section of the *House of Fame* is interesting as one of Chaucer's few excursions into fully developed personification allegory, and elsewhere I have suggested the *Ovide Moralisé* as a likely source for his unique portrait of Fame as judge.[1] But the purpose of the judgment scene is obvious. It restates allegorically the point that has already been made in other ways: that tradition, or fame, is no reliable guide to factual truth. Moreover, while the judgment scene forms the dramatic center of Book 3, it is not Geffrey's only source of enlightenment as to the real nature of fame. If the ambivalence of tradition has been revealed in the Proem and the first two books, the fickleness of Fame personified is made obvious to Geffrey from the moment he sets foot in her realm. This is managed through the iconography of Fame's palace, some of which is explicitly interpreted, and some of which makes its statement only symbolically.

1. In "Chaucer's *House of Fame* and the *Ovide Moralisé*," *Comparative Literature* 20 (1968).

The iconography of Fame's palace has long been recognized as conventional; many a house of Fortune, that other variant goddess, resembles the place that Geffrey sees.[2] Geffrey notices first that the building stands on a mountain of ice, and his interpretation of this detail leaves no doubt that he is already aware of Fame's deficiencies.

> Thoughte I, "By seynt Thomas of Kent!
> This were a feble fundament
> To bilden on a place hye.
> He ought him lytel glorifye
> That hereon bilt, God so me save!"
>
> *(1131–35)*

The reflection may point to a Boethian passage (*De Consolatione Philosophiae*, 2, met. 4) in which Philosophy describes the building of a "perdurable seete" in contrast to the ill-founded palace of worldly ambition. Or it may derive from the biblical parable of the foolish and wise men who build their houses respectively on sand and on stone (Matt. 7: 24–27). Whatever its source, the interpretation indicates that Geffrey is far less puzzled by his environment here than he was at the beginning of Book 2. And later he comments in an equally knowledgeable way on the walls of the palace; these are made of beryl

> That shoone ful lyghter than a glas
> And made wel more than hit was
> To semen every thing, ywis,
> As kynde thyng of Fames is . . . .
>
> *(1289–92)*

Well before the judgment scene, then, Geffrey's remarks on what he sees suggest that he understands fame and is prepared to evaluate it correctly.

---

2. See W. O. Sypherd, *Studies in Chaucer's House of Fame* (London, 1907), pp. 17, 114–18; Howard R. Patch, *The Goddess Fortuna* (Cambridge, Mass., 1927), p. 110.

Geffrey does not explicitly interpret everything he sees. But the figures he notices and names are as much part of the iconography of Fame as the more traditional features of her palace. Some of these figures are not only famous but the subject of dual fame, as Aeneas was in Book 1. Some, if not themselves ambivalent, are made to participate in an ironic interplay by virtue of their placement in the poem. Still others serve the cause of Fame in various ways that permit us to construct a complete idea of her character. Together these figures reinforce the skeptical attitude toward tradition that has been established in earlier sections of the poem.

The first figure named by Geffrey is Orpheus, chief of the many musicians who occupy niches built into the palace walls. As the archetypal singer of classical tradition, Orpheus represents poets at large and therefore poetry itself. It is interesting, then, that Orpheus possessed a reputation as divided as that of Aeneas—a reputation whose duality reflects the ambivalence of poetic tradition itself. In many allegorical interpretations of classical myth, Orpheus is said to represent the divinely inspired faculty of reason. Robert Holcot (d. 1349), the Cambridge theologian, calls Orpheus "theologus et musicus incomparabilis."[3] Boccaccio describes him as the man whose wisdom and eloquence can move even hardened sinners to return to the path of virtue (*Genealogia*, 5. 12); and Dante gives a similar interpretation of Orpheus in the *Convivio* (2. 1). Because of his divine inspiration and his journey to the underworld, Orpheus sometimes appears as a type of Christ. In such interpretations, Orpheus's wife, Eurydice, becomes a symbol of the sinful soul whom Christ seeks here below (see the *Ovide Moralisé*, 10. 396–407).

At the same time, an opposite interpretation had developed. Since Orpheus was popularly believed to have become homosexual in disappointment over the loss of

---

3. From a sermon of Holcot, printed in Beryl Smalley, *English Friars and Antiquity in the Early Fourteenth Century* (Oxford, 1960), p. 60.

Eurydice, he was often taken as a symbol of unnatural lust. This tradition, like the other, was so widespread that Chaucer can hardly have been unaware of it. It occurs in texts he is known to have used, including the *Roman de la Rose* (19642 ff.) and the *Ovide Moralisé* (10. 206–19)— the latter, with that fine disregard for consistency made possible by allegorical exegesis, now condemns Orpheus for his perversion. A similar view glosses Orpheus's final loss of his wife as the weak soul's uncontrollable desire for earthly things: just as Orpheus cannot help looking back at his wife as they ascend from hell, so men look back on their sinful ways and forfeit their souls in reminiscence. This interpretation appears in Trivet's commentary on Boethius, and Chaucer incorporated it into his own translation of *De Consolatione Philosophiae* (3, met. 12). Orpheus's double reputation illustrates the fickleness of fame that has already been suggested by conventional iconography and is soon to be demonstrated in action.

After Orpheus and other major musicians, Geffrey notices thousands of minor musicians and magicians. Some of them are famous; some, through their art, have caused others to be famous. Many of these artists and conjurers deal in illusion, and their skill, like fame itself, may serve a good or evil purpose ("To make a man ben hool or syk," 1270).

On entering the castle gate, Geffrey encounters crowds of people begging the benefits of Fame. Among them is a group of those "that crien riche folkes laudes," each decorated with the arms of the family whose fame he has disseminated. The enormous wealth associated with these "pursevaunts and heraudes" suggests that flattery and bribery may well have had a place in their particular duties. This vision of wealth generates a brief description of the richness of Fame's palace, plated half a foot thick with gold and studded with jewels. While it is true that any otherworldly edifice in medieval literature is liable to be described as surrealistically rich, still the Narrator reverts to this point so often here (in lines 1306, 1315–19, 1327, 1341–55, 1356,

1362, 1393–94) that we are led to connect it with Fame's very nature, to conclude that fame can be bought and that great wealth generates its own fame.

Geffrey now has his first view of the goddess herself, and there follows a description of her based mainly on *Aeneid* 4. 73–97. Fame is surrounded by wealth and by the sound of her own praise. On her shoulders she bears

> Both th'armes and the name
> Of thoo that hadde large fame:
> Alexander and Hercules . . . .
> *(1411–13)*

Together these heroes provide a balanced comment on the nature and limits of human achievement. The point is not that these heroes are equally famous—in fact Alexander, a central figure in the medieval popular tradition, looms far larger than Hercules in importance. Their presence here— like their arms—is emblematic, and if we are to appreciate the moral force of that emblem we must turn again to the literary tradition.

In chivalric romances, Alexander is sometimes mentioned as the model of *largesse*, one of the foremost courtly and chivalric virtues. But far more dominant is the use of Alexander as an example of pride and ambition, as a medieval overreacher who must be taught the lesson of humility (see above, chapter 7). In the various Alexander texts, that lesson is administered in many different ways: in the teaching of a mysterious old man; by direct intervention of the gods; in a letter from Alexander's tutor, Aristotle; by Alexander's enemies; in documents, conversations, or dreams.

The reputation of Hercules, on the other hand, is (with almost no exceptions) consistently virtuous. He is admired as an example of the virtue of fortitude, the moral strength symbolized by his physical prowess. Often he is portrayed as a type of Christ in both literary and graphic art,[4] and the

4. Marcel Simon, *Hercule et le Christianisme* (Paris, 1955). Seznec notes that from the thirteenth century Hercules was the protector and symbol of the city of Florence (p. 20 n.). And B. G. Koonce, attempting

Ovide Moralisé regularly refers to him as "Diex li glorieuz vainquerres." Indeed so strong is the will to preserve the good name of Hercules that this text favorably explicates even his adultery and subsequent perversion, when he and his mistress Iole exchange clothing and roles; both of these episodes are said to represent God's incarnation (9. 873–901). Boethius provides a list of Hercules' heroic labors, together with an exhortation to men to emulate this model. The exhortation and Chaucer's gloss on it read:

> Goth now thanne, ye stronge men, ther as the heye wey of the greet ensaumple ledith yow. O nyce men! why nake ye your bakkes? *(As who seith, "O ye slowe and delicat men! whi flee ye adversites, and ne fyghte nat ayeins hem by vertu, to wynnen the mede of the hevens?")* For the erthe overcomen yeveth the sterres. *(This to seyn, that whan that erthly lust is overcomyn, a man is makid worthy to the hevene.)*
>
> *(4, metrum 7)*

Alexander as ruler of the world exercised an exploitative, that is, a political, power; whereas Hercules in his labors was distinguished for a strength which he used to benefit, not control, other people. Alexander was often tempted to transcend the normal limits of power and knowledge, whereas Hercules' strength, though extraordinary, did not tempt him to abuse it. Moreover the Alexander tradition itself links the names of two heroes in a way which proves that their juxtaposition in the *House of Fame* is not accidental. One of Alexander's best-known adventures is his journey to the eastern pillars of Hercules. These boundaries Hercules had set up to mark the point beyond which men ought not to pass; earlier he had placed the "pillars of Hercules" at Gibraltar to mark the western limits of exploration. In many versions, Alexander strikes down the eastern gates in order to surpass the achievements of the

---

to demonstrate the "tainted pagan glory" of Hercules, is unable to adduce a single unequivocal example of Hercules' bad name (*Chaucer and the Tradition of Fame*, p. 214).

mythic hero; but the gods are so angry at this transgression that Alexander is soon made to restore the pillars. In view of this connection, then, Hercules as a setter of limits and Alexander as a trespasser of limits form a pair with implications sufficiently important to warrant their being supported by Fame herself. Indeed they provide a comment upon Fame, for to be famous is to exercise a kind of power, and power is a guarantee of fame. Beyond this, the poet's use of fame (tradition) confers on him, as we have seen in chapter 6, a particular power which, like physical or political power, may be used in a reckless and exploitative way or for benevolent ends. The presence of Alexander and Hercules reminds us of those possibilities, which, having been suggested emblematically, are now to be illustrated from the historical tradition itself.

Geffrey turns his attention again to his surroundings at Fame's court. He observes a double colonnade of metal pillars extending the length of the hall; on each pillar is the figure of an author bearing the fame of his subject. Of these, Chaucer names and describes twelve, who among them provide a conspectus of medieval historical tradition. Although the authors do not appear in chronological sequence, the subjects they support are arranged in three periods thought by medieval scholars to be roughly chronological: Jewish (represented by Josephus), Greek (Statius, Homer, Dares and Dictys, "Lollius," Guido delle Colonne, Geoffrey of Monmouth[5]), and Roman (Virgil, Ovid, Lucan, Claudian). Nearly all of these writers were familiar school authors whose works were part of the arts curriculum, were anthologized in *florilegia,* and were regularly used as sources for historical and encyclopedic compilations.[6]

5. Geoffrey of Monmouth does not treat the Trojan War directly, but in narrating the fortunes of Aeneas's descendants and their ultimate arrival in Britain he does provide an epilogue to the matter of Troy.

6. For Chaucer's knowledge of classical and other writers, see T. R. Lounsbury, *Studies in Chaucer* (London, 1892), vol. 2, chap. 5; and Eleanor Hammond's *Bibliographical Manual* (New York, 1908, reprinted 1933), pp. 84–105.

Historians and poets alike appear in the group, for Chaucer, like most of his contemporaries, does not always distinguish between poetry and historical chronicle—the two kinds of narrative in which tradition was handed down.

Like the other personae already encountered, the famous authors form an integral part of the iconography of Fame. They constitute a composite portrait of historical authority, which is revealed to be fully as contradictory as the literary authorities used in Book 1, or the cosmologies of Book 2. Contradiction in some cases inheres in the subject matter; in other cases it emerges from comparison of several authors whose juxtaposition in the poem provides a mutual critique. This vision of uncertainty anticipates the judgment scene in preparing us for the whimsical decisions of Fame. It stands in relation to that scene as effect to cause, for from existing historical tradition we move to an imaginative reconstruction of the process by which that tradition was made.

First among the authors is Josephus, whose best known works were the *Antiquities* (a history of the Jews from creation to the start of the war with Rome), and *The Jewish War* (an account of Jewish struggles from the time of Juda Maccabee to the destruction of the Temple in A.D. 70). Chaucer seems to refer to both works when he notes that the Jewish tradition includes

> batayles,
> As wel as other olde mervayles.
> *(1441–42)*

The historical Jewry represented by Josephus can only have had a divided reputation for a medieval audience. Judaism was, to be sure, generally acknowledged to be the forerunner of Christianity, and in vernacular literature three Jewish heroes—Joshua, David, and Juda Maccabee— were included among the Nine Worthies. But the doctrinal source of hostility is clearly stated by Augustine, who claims that

> if they [the Jews] had not sinned against Him with
> impious curiosity, which seduced them like magic
> arts, and drew them to strange gods and idols, and
> at last led them to kill Christ, their kingdom would
> have remained to them, and would have been, if
> not more spacious, yet more happy than that of
> Rome.[7]

Augustine's relatively moderate tone was by no means
typical of the many anti-Jewish polemics that were attributed to him during the Middle Ages or of the tracts written
by such well-known scholars as Tertullian, Isidore of Seville, Peter Damian, William of Auvergne, and a host of
minor and anonymous authors. It was the notion of "rep-
robate Jews" that came to dominate the medieval popular
imagination: the *Ovide Moralisé,* interpreting Caesar's
death as a figure of Christ's death, reflects the popular view
of "li faus juif plain de fallace." Secular persecution was of
course common throughout Europe. It consisted in special
taxes on Jews, their exclusion from normal civil and political life, and periodic massacres of entire communities.
Pogroms were especially frequent during the fourteenth
century, when Jews were often held responsible for the
plague that recurrently swept Europe. Nor, in evaluating
the late medieval attitude toward Jews, can one ignore the
role of the Inquisition in perpetuating anti-Semitic feeling,
for the Inquisition legitimized the burning of Jewish books
and the persecution of Jews and of those who tried to pro-
tect them or their literature. Precisely what Chaucer
thought of such actions is not clear. That he was acquainted
with them we know from the *Prioresse's Tale,* which tells of
a ritual murder by Jews, of the victim's miraculous res-
urrection and the subsqumt persecution of the Jewish
community. As usual, Chaucer does not explicitly commit
himself, allowing his own irony and the Prioress's sentimentality to shape our response. But Josephus and the
Prioresse's Tale mark the extreme points of a single tradi-

7. *The City of God,* 4: 34, trans. Thomas Merton (New York, 1950).

tion, and the popular anti-Semitic miracle is as relevant to the fame of Jewry as the scholarly chronicle. Fame has chosen to perpetuate both, for, as she remarks of herself, there is "in me no justice."

The next seven writers form a group by virtue of having perpetuated the fame of Greek heroes in the Theban war and in "the matter of Troy." Statius is named first,

> That bar of Thebes up the fame
> Upon his shuldres, and the name
> Also of cruel Achilles.
>
> *(1461–63)*

—that is, as author of the *Thebaid* and the *Achilleid*. There is a certain irony in the epithet applied to Achilles here, for the *Achilleid* is essentially a romantic comedy. It tells of the efforts of Thetis to keep her son out of the Trojan war, of Achilles' female disguise and his concealment at the court of Lycomedes, his seduction of the princess Deidamia, and his final discovery through the ruses of Ulysses and Diomedes. The accessus to one medieval manuscript of the work states: "Moralitas enim consistit in sollicitudine matris erga filium et in obediencia filii erga matrem"[8]—a *moralitas* at odds not only with the Narrator's characterization of Achilles as "cruel," but with the portrait of Achilles that is presented by Homer.

That sort of ironic tension is made more explicit in the rest of the passage, which describes the other authors in the group and their literary quarrels:

> And by him [i.e., Statius] stood, withouten les,
> Ful wonder hy on a piler
> Of yren, he, the gret Omer;
> And with him Dares and Tytus
> Before, and eke he Lollius,
> And Guydo eke de Columpnis,

---

8. The manuscript, together with its accessus, is edited in Paul Clogan, "Chaucer and the Medieval Statius" (Ph.D. diss., University of Illinois, 1961).

And Englyssh Gaufride eke, ywis;
And ech of these, as have I joye,
Was besy for to bere up Troye.
So hevy therof was the fame
That for to bere hyt was no game.
But yet I gan ful wel espie,
Betwex hem was a litil envye.
Oon seyde that Omer made lyes,
Feynynge in hys poetries,
And was to Grekes favorable;
Therfor held he hyt but fable.

(1464–80)

Besides Homer, the earliest sources for the matter of Troy were two translations of forged Greek "eyewitness" accounts. One, the *Ephemeris Belli Troiani,* dating from about the fourth century, claimed to be the military diary of a Greek soldier in the war, Dictys Cretensis ("Tytus"). The other, the *De Excidio Troiae Historia,* was a sixth-century translation of a work supposedly by a Trojan soldier, Dares Phrygius. These two sources drew on and perpetuated a long-standing anti-Homeric tradition which, largely through their efforts, became a medieval tradition as well. They and others rejected the authenticity of Homer on the grounds that he was no contemporary of the events he describes, that he was naturally partial to his countrymen, that he blasphemously showed the gods in combat with mortals, and showed the gods to be of bad character as well. Both Dares and Dictys exalt characters whom Homer treats as minor, deprecate or minimize the roles of the great Homeric heroes, and, in an attempt to reduce the epic machinery, omit or provide alternate explanations for various supernatural interventions. Later treatments of the material handle the problem of conflicting sources in different ways. Benoit de Saint-Maure, author of the twelfth-century *Roman de Troie,* comes down firmly on the side of the "eyewitness" accounts (*Troie,* 45–128). Imitating Benoit's reliance on Dares and Dictys, Guido delle Colonne states that his own *Historia Troiana* (1287) is intended as a corrective to the errors not of Homer alone but of Virgil and Ovid also, who had followed Homer ("liber ultimus"). The anonymous author of the *Ovide Moralisé*, after discussing the problem at some length, excuses Homer on the grounds that "il parla par metaphore," and leaves the final discussion to his reader (12. 1719–54).

Contradiction had been inherent in the Troy tradition from the beginning, and in the lines cited above Chaucer repeats the substance of the early charges against Homer. He offers no personal opinion on the matter, and since he has no sure way of evaluating the traditional material, he simply presents what he has received. Given the nature of the tradition, though, no opinion could be more damaging than that simple presentation.

The presence of Dares and Dictys in the catalogue of authors obviously undercuts the authority of Homer. It does the same with Virgil, supporter of "pius Aeneas," who is named directly after the accusation against Homer. The anti-Homeric tradition portrays Aeneas, with Antenor, as an archtraitor to his people, susceptible to bribery and profiting from the destruction of his city. That tradition survives in the opening lines of *Gawain and the Green Knight:*

> The tulk that the trammes of tresoun ther wroght
> Was tried for his tricherie, the trewest on erthe.
> Hit was Ennias the athel and his highe kynde
> That sithen depreced provinces. . . .[9]

9. There has been some difference of opinion concerning the identity of the "tulk . . . tried for treason." In his edition of *Gawain* (EETS, no. 210 [1940]), Sir Israel Gollancz claimed that the reference is to Antenor. A. C. Cawley's edition (London, 1962) follows Gollancz; so does Marie Borroff in her translation (New York, 1967).
I think it is pointless to bring in Antenor, an unnamed character, when Aeneas, named in line 5, is entirely adequate. Aeneas was a traitor in the anti-Homeric tradition, and he was also tried for treachery (by the Greeks). Literary structure argues for Aeneas since it is Aeneas's descendants, not Antenor's, who were said to have settled Britain. I have therefore accepted as correct the reading of Madden (Bannatyne Club, 1839) and of Tolkien and Gordon (Oxford, 1925).

Virgil is followed by Ovid, whose portrait of Aeneas in the *Heroides* is that of a fickle seducer of women. Thus the placement of Virgil between these two major critics of Aeneas—Ovid and the anti-Homerites—illustrates the ironic possibilities of juxtaposition as a structural technique.

The reputation of Julius Caesar, whose fame Lucan supports, was also a subject of particular debate among medieval scholars. During the late thirteenth and fourteenth centuries this debate was not only due to a proliferation of literary opinion. It also reflected the extraordinary social ferment of the time and especially the rapid changes in class structure that had occurred throughout Europe. Frederick Antal notes that late medieval evaluations of Caesar and Brutus, "even within the classicising range of ideas," depended on the writer's class loyalty. Thus Leonardo Bruni (1369–1444), historian and champion of upper middle-class liberties, "was against the 'tyrant' Caesar and on the side of Brutus, his tyrant's murderer. . . . Dante, the Ghibelline, banished Brutus into lowest Hell; Petrarch, with his emotional Roman republicanism, praised him. The conservative Salutati [Coluccio Salutati, 1331–1406], who was most concerned for the maintenance of the existing order, was . . . again on Caesar's side."[10] Those who condemned the assassination of Caesar had Augustine on their side, for he had cited the event as one sign among many of the internal corruption of the Roman Empire (*City of God*, 3. 30). Later scholars, blaming Caesar as a tyrant, viewed his murder as a sign of political health; their task was to adjust Augustine's judgment to the requirements of nascent bourgeois liberty and anti-imperial sentiment.[11]

Lucan portrays Caesar as a monster of egotism, hypocrisy, and treachery. Chaucer probably knew Lucan's

10. *Florentine Painting and Its Social Background* (London, 1948), p. 63, n. 71. See also E. Schanzer, "Dante and Julius Caesar," *Medium Aevum* 24 (1955).

11. For a brief discussion of the later Caesar tradition, see Smalley, *English Friars*, pp. 126–28, 315–18.

Pharsalia directly, or at least parts of it. Most other texts which he knew did not, however, follow Lucan's bias. Ovid's *Metamorphoses* ends with a panegyric on Caesar and his adopted son Augustus (15. 745ff.), which, in the *Ovide Moralisé,* is predictably interpreted as a figural anticipation of God the Father and Jesus (7177ff.). Even "selonc l'estorie," the *Ovide Moralisé* describes Caesar as the model knight:

> Larges donneres, bons guerriers
> Fu et preus et chevalereus,
> Sages et si bateillereus
> Que riens ne duroit vers s'espee.
> *(15. 7030–33)*

Li Hystore de Julius Cesar, a thirteenth-century prose redaction of the *Pharsalia,* presents Pompey as a deserving victim of Fortune's wheel, while Caesar is an exemplary figure who "fist tant et cunkist, par le viertut de nostre seignour premierement et par se proueche en apries."[12] Though Chaucer cites Lucan only as bearer of Caesar's and Pompey's fame, he can scarcely have overlooked the importance of the *Pharsalia* as a work which attempts to undercut not only its own major characters but epic conventions and the epic past. Its skepticism toward portents and omens, oracles and visions; its cynical treatment of classical myth; its sardonic deprecation of the once-great landmarks of Troy when Caesar visits the home of his ancestor Aeneas (Book 9)—these are obvious blows against the Virgilian tradition. We may see Lucan, then, not only as a critic of Caesar, but as a critic of Virgil too, his presence a silent, ironic commentary on the hero whose "fame" he upholds and on the greatest poet of the story of Troy.

Were Claudian, last author in the group of nine, brought forth as the author of political poems, his relation to the other authors would be clear: his praise of Rome and her

---

12. Jehane de Tuim, *Li Hystore de Julius César,* ed. F. Settegast (Halle, 1881), Prologue, p. 2. F. N. Robinson notes that in the *Man of Law's Tale,* line 400, the reference is probably to the *Hystore.*

rulers might have helped to restore the balance that has been upset by several critics of the Roman past. Instead, Claudian appears as bearer of the fame of hell—that is, as author of the narrative poem *De Raptu Proserpinae.* We may note in Chaucer's description that the pillar of sulfur on which Claudian stands is iconographically inaccurate, for there is no sulfur in Claudian's underworld.[13] Indeed the kingdom to which Pluto abducts Proserpina is not altogether unpleasant, for, like other classical versions of the underworld, it is the abode of all the dead, not merely of sinners.

> There a richer age, a golden race has its home, and we possess forever what men win but once. Soft meads shall fail thee not, and ever-blooming flowers, such as thy Henna ne'er produced, breathe to gentler zephyrs. There is, moreover, a precious tree in the leafy groves whose curving branches gleam with living ore—a tree consecrate to thee. Thou shalt be queen of blessed autumn and ever enriched with golden fruit.[14]

Thus Pluto addresses Proserpina, "that quene is of the derke pyne" (1512). With this brief but pregnant reminder of life after death—the telos of every personal history and of Christian collective history—Chaucer closes his survey of historical authorities.

Fame's judgment now follows, showing the process whose product—written history—we have just encountered. As soon as the ninth company has received its deserved ill fame, a fellow bystander addresses the Narrator: "Artow come hider to han fame?" (1872). "Nay, for sothe, frend," answers Geffrey, letting his interjection serve also

13. Robert Pratt notes, however, that sulfur does appear elsewhere in Claudian's poem: in the description of Mount Aetna, whence Proserpina was abducted ("Chaucer's Claudian," *Speculum* 22 [1943]). The notion of hell as a sulfurous place inhabited by demons is a Christian development.

14. "The Rape of Proserpina," 2. 282–302, trans. M. Platnauer in *Claudian* (Cambridge, Mass., 1922), Loeb series, no. 136, vol. 2.

as a statement of purpose. Without hesitation Geffrey dissociates himself from the scene he has just witnessed:

> "I cam noght hyder, graunt mercy,
> For no such cause, by my hed!
> Sufficeth me, as I were ded,
> That no wight have my name in honde.
> I wot myself best how y stonde;
> For what I drye, or what I thynke,
> I wil myselven al hyt drynke,
> Certeyn, for the more part,
> As fer forth as I kan myn art."
>
> (1874–82)

In this cryptic manifesto, the core of Book 3, Geffrey's corrective to the delusive search for fame is a reassertion of subjective judgment, though it is a qualified reassertion. The artist hopes that his name will not be abused and claims to know best what his merit is ("how I stonde"). Geffrey does not conclude that his fame will be proportional to his merit. Instead he puts aside the entire question of reputation with the tautological statement that insofar as he is able to create and to judge his creation ("As fer forth as I kan myn art"), to that degree he is able to take responsibility for himself.

The apparent independence asserted here should not be read as a rejection on Geffrey's part of his earlier submission to divine authority. On the contrary, the limited independence claimed here is based precisely on the experience of the Proem and first two books, for it does not reject Christian doctrine but literary tradition as a guide: in this case, though, the tradition of the future. At this point in the poem Geffrey and Chaucer seem to speak in the same voice, for both of them are practicing poets who will soon become part of the literary past. Every poem Geffrey writes brings him closer, whether he will or not, to being part of that same vast, multivalent tradition in which he works. As a poet, Geffrey can hardly avoid fame. Whether it will be good or bad fame he can neither know nor control.

To write well will not guarantee him good fame, so that all he can consciously do is strive for truth in his work—a hazardous job, as we have already seen, and not lightly undertaken.

His credo thus established, Geffrey is asked by the same rightly curious bystander to justify his presence at Fame's court. Geffrey's answer reminds us of the original motive for this cosmic journey. It also repeats the self-deprecating irony we have noticed before, for Jove's reward has been sadly disappointing, and Geffrey has learned nothing new so far.

> "For certeynly, he that me made
> To comen hyder, seyde me,
> Y shulde bothe here and se,
> In this place, wonder thynges;
> But these be no suche tydynges
> As I mene of." "Noo?" quod he.
> And I answered, "Noo, parde!
> For wel y wiste ever yit,
> Sith that first y hadde wit,
> That somme folk han desired fame
> Diversly, and loos, and name. . . ."
>   (*1890–1900*)

The Narrator's disappointment here resembles his earlier frustration on leaving the Temple of Venus. Once again the narrative grinds to a halt and fails to generate further action. The allegorical set piece of Fame's judgment has proved as static and infertile as the story of Aeneas and Dido. The Narrator needs to be rescued, and so does his story.

That service the anonymous interrogator now performs (as the Eagle did before) by escorting Geffrey to a new locus. It is the House of Rumor, more marvellously constructed than Dedalus' labyrinth, whirling eternally, and full of talk of whatever happens on earth. This, it seems, is Geffrey's real destination. It has at least—what Fame's palace had not—the merit of rousing his curiosity and his desire to participate in the local action. Spying his Eagle perched nearby on a stone, Geffrey asks for a delay so that he can take advantage of this last opportunity to learn something valuable:

> "For yit, paraunter, y may lere
> Som good thereon, or sumwhat here
> That leef me were, or that y wente."
>
> *(1997–99)*

The Eagle agrees willingly, takes Geffrey once more "up bitween hys toon," and deposits him in the place where, finally, the promised tidings may be heard.

THE HOUSE OF RUMOR

The structural relation between Fame's palace and the House of Rumor is clear enough. All tidings originate in the House of Rumor, but they fly to Fame's court to be judged and dispersed:

> Thus out at holes gunne wringe
> Every tydynge streght to Fame,
> And she gan yeven ech hys name,
> After hir disposicioun,
> And yaf hem eke duracioun,
> Somme to wexe and wane sone,
> As doth the faire white mone,
> And let hem goon.
>
> *(2110–17)*

The inhabitants of Fame's palace, it will be remembered, are historical or legendary figures, long dead. Even the crowds of petitioners have been resurrected in order to show how good or bad eminence, or no eminence at all, has been achieved in the past. None of the petitioners at Fame's palace has any independent significance, and we are given no information about them other than that which relates to their iconographical function as append-ages to Fame. The House of Rumor, on the other hand, is populated with crowds whose exclusive concern is the present. Many of them have occupations which make them appropriate retailers of news: shipmen and pilgrims, pardoners, couriers, messengers. All of them are actively engaged in the business of life, or at least in talking about it, and their interests include whatever is temporal and temporary. Yet despite this wholehearted dedication to the present in the House of Rumor, the scene is a portrait of history in the making. It is a vision of the present as history, for what it shows is the raw material of tradition. At Fame's palace Geffrey was able to observe the process by which the past becomes known to, or hidden from, the present; conversely, the House of Rumor reveals the present fast becoming history.

In several ways the reader's understanding of fame is augmented by Geffrey's experience at the House of Rumor. We see, first, that the matter narrated by historical and literary authorities was once the stuff of daily life, that before being transmuted into art it was no more than the usual succession

> Of werres, of pes, of mariages,
> Of reste, of labour, of viages,
> Of abood, of deeth, of lyf,
> Of love, of hate, acord, of stryfe,
> Of loos, of lore, and of wynnynges,
> Of hele, of seknesse, or bildynges,
> Of faire wyndes, and of tempestes,
> Of qwalm of folk, and eke of bestes;
> Of dyvers transmutacions
> Of estats, and eke of regions;
> Of trust, of drede, of jelousye,
> Of wit, of wynnynge, of folye;
> Of plente, and of gret famyne,
> Of chepe, of derthe, and of ruyne;
> Of good or mys governement,
> Of fyr, and of dyvers accident.
> *(1961–76)*

It is pertinent to recall here that "history" has two meanings which closely parallel the two meanings of "fame." Just as fame signifies contemporary rumor and traditional renown, so history may be simply the rehearsing of certain memorable deeds—as in *Li Hystore de Julius Cesar* or Abelard's *Historia Calamitatum Meum*—or it may be a systematic account of the human past, as in the *Speculum Historiale* of Vincent of Beauvais. In the movement of tidings from the House of Rumor to Fame's palace, we see histories becoming history, and rumor becoming renown. Chaucer as a courtier was especially well placed to observe this process, especially when the industrious and inquisitive Froissart was present at court to remind him of it.

In the allegory of Fame's judgment, Fame is the agent by which tradition is made from facts. But both we and Geffrey are aware that in reality the individual writer is responsible for making something permanent of tidings. "I praye who schulde now knowe emperours," demands Ralph Higden, the monk of Chester,

> wonder of philosophres, other folwe the apostles, but hir noble dedes and hir wonder workes were i-writ in stories and so i-kept in mynde? Who schulde knowe Lucilium, but Seneca in his pistles hadde i-write his dedes? Writing of poetes is more worthy of preisynge of emperoures than al the welthe of this worlde, and ryches that they welde while that they were a lyve. For story is wytnesse of tyme, mynde of lyf, messager of eldnesse; story weldeth passyng doynges, story putteth forthe hir professoures. Dedes that wolde be lost story ruleth; dedes that wolde flee out of mynde, story clepeth agen; dedes that wolde deie, story kepeth hem evermore.
>
> *(Bk. 1, chap. 1, "Prologus")*

So that it is not only Geffrey's own fame that depends on himself, as he has already said in his credo (1873–82), but also the perpetuation of his matter. This is not stated explicitly, but we have already seen the rows of authors bearing up their subjects to remind us that tradition depends on its transmitters. Now we are brought to the source of it all, for the House of Rumor shows us the makings of the poet's fame and of his subject's fame: the daily facts that constitute his real poetic material. That this, rather than tradition itself, is Geffrey's true interest, is suggested by the change in his behavior. His earlier detachment from the action at Fame's palace is replaced by eager participation:

> I alther-fastest wente
> About, and dide al myn entente
> Me for to pleyen and for to lere,
> And eke a tydynge for to here. . .
> *(2131–34)*

The incompleteness of the *House of Fame* does not, I think, pose the kind of problem which can be solved by conjecture about the identity of the "man of gret auctorite," with whose appearance the work ends. Such speculation adds nothing to a narrative poem which seems to lack only a few lines, and whose main ideas and methods are already clear. Whatever the identity of the anonymous figure, his message, had it been delivered, could only have intensified an already existing structural paradox. Chaucer has amply demonstrated the unreliability or ambivalence of traditional statements, and through continual ironic undercutting of conventional devices he has encouraged the reader to receive such statements with skepticism. It is difficult to imagine any figure of authority sufficient to overcome the impact of the rest of the poem, short of Christ himself—and neither the tone nor the subject matter of the poem suggests an apocalyptic vision.

As a literary statement about the unreliability of literary statements, then, the *House of Fame* tends to render itself superfluous, not unlike the Cretan who claims all Cretans to be liars. This paradox is not limited to literature, for we have already observed (above in chapter 2) how the "leap of faith" in some late medieval philosophy limited the exercise of logic to matters of contingency, insuring that logic would not step beyond its "proper" limits to deny the existence of what was thought to lie beyond those limits. Nor is this paradox confined to the Middle Ages, and Engels' critique of Hegelian philosophy diagnoses the flaw at the heart of any version of skeptical fideism:

> It was suffering, in fact, from an internal and incurable contradiction. Upon the one hand, its essential proposition was the conception that human history is a process of evolution, which, by its very nature, cannot find its intellectual final term in the discovery of any so-called absolute truth. But, on the other hand, it laid claim to being the very essence of this absolute truth.
>
> *(Socialism: Utopian and Scientific)*

In the sense that its inner contradiction cannot be resolved in the terms set up in the poem, the *House of Fame* is an unfinishable work, and nothing in it proclaims Chaucer's dilemma so well as the absence of an ending.

In earlier chapters I have noted that at certain points in the *House of Fame* the experience of the Narrator—who is himself a poet—closely approaches Chaucer's. This seems especially true at the end of Book 1, where the Narrator prays for protection from phantom, and again in Book 3, where he states his credo. Such passages do not, of course, mean that the *House of Fame* is an autobiographical allegory which can be connected at every point with some fact of Chaucer's life. They do suggest, though, that Chaucer used the work to explore some artistic problems with which he was directly concerned. The Narrator's progression from Fame's palace to the House of Rumor has sometimes been identified as a key episode in Chaucer's statement of artistic intention. It has been said to represent his rejection of allegory and other conventional material in favor of the more "realistic" kinds of action and character that were to be portrayed in the *Canterbury Tales*.[15] I would suggest that the premise of this interpretation is correct but that its conclusion is not. Surely Chaucer is saying something, in this last episode, about literary tradition and personal experience, but I doubt that he is committing himself to experience at the expense of tradition. Allegory is not, after all, absent from the *Canterbury Tales*: there is the *Tale of Melibee*, the *Clerk's Tale*, the *Man of Law's Tale*—all of them probably later than the *House of Fame*—and the overall symbolic implications of pilgrimage itself as suggested in the *Parson's Prologue* (X. 1, 48—51). Chaucer's work during or shortly after the period of composition of the *House of Fame* also includes the translation of Boethius's allegorical dialogue, the *De Consolatione Philosophiae*. And even in the *House of Fame* itself there is no overall progression from allegory to other techniques, for the nature of fame, or tradition, has been demonstrated from the start of the poem in a variety of nonallegorical ways.

What, then, is the meaning of the House of Rumor? One ought not, I think, violate the structure of Book 3 by considering the House of Rumor in isolation and apart from Fame's court, to which it is closely related. Indeed, Fame's court could not exist without the House of Rumor, for there originate the events which fame either commemorates or condemns to oblivion. Plainly the House of Rumor and Fame's court—the loci, respectively, of experience and of literary tradition—are not antithetical but complementary. Experience, mediated through art, generates tradition; tradition helps us to evaluate experience. Neither locus is

15. This view is implied in several early autobiographical interpretations of the *House of Fame*, for example, that of Bernard ten Brink. For a discussion of some of these theories, see Sypherd, *Studies*, pp. 156–60. A similar view is offered by R. C. Goffin, "Quiting by Tidings in the *House of Fame*," *Medium Aevum* 12 (1943).

absolute; not only are the two related, but both are subject to contingency or chance. Fame's palace is built on a mountain of ice (1124–35)—"a feble fundament"—and the House of Rumor is built of twigs:

> Al was the tymber of no strengthe,
> Yet hit is founded to endure
> While that hit lyst to Aventure,
> That is the moder of tydynges.
> *(1980–83)*

Chance ("Aventure"), mother of the tidings that circulate in the House of Rumor, can choose when she pleases to destroy the House of Rumor; she is as whimsical as Fame. Chaucer seems to be saying of the world of experience that its survival is not absolutely reliable. (Contemporary philosophers were saying something quite similar: that in view of God's absolute freedom and power nothing in the phenomenal world can escape contingency.) When we recall further that true and false tidings fly together from the windows of the House of Rumor (2088–2109), we must acknowledge that the House of Rumor, with its wealth of worldly experience, is no more reliable—in the absolute sense—a source of information than the palace of Fame. This is the depth of Chaucer's skepticism. Experience is no substitute for tradition for it is subject to the same weakness: neither can be relied on for truth. To this final statement of the skeptical dilemma, no fideistic solution is offered; none, I think, could convincingly serve.

Chaucer's Narrator has learned something, in Book 3, about the limits of tradition and experience. An ending might have included some explicit statement about their relation, but even without an ending it seems clear that no choice is required between the two places of Book 3, because neither is distinctly superior to the other. At Fame's court and at the House of Rumor the Narrator can and does find something to occupy his attention; each place provides something that the other cannot. If the Narrator is committed to anything he is committed to pluralism. That, I suggest, is the closest Chaucer comes to a statement of his own literary intentions, and it is amply borne out in the work that was to follow.

Epilogue: Looking Forward

Like the philosopher's "leap of faith," Chaucer's experiment with skeptical fideism in the *House of Fame* brought a certain freedom. The poem poses the problem of choice among conflicting traditions—the problem of truth in art—and it shows such choice to be impossible and unnecessary. The artist is therefore released from the obligation to make explicit choices in his art, for he has committed himself instead to the ultimate truth of faith, which shows all else to be relative: all historical, scientific and perceptual "truth" to be, after all, unreliable. Poetic material in the *House of Fame* is presented to the Narrator as an object of choice: dream as inspiration or disorder, Virgil's Aeneas or Ovid's, classical science or classical myth. That the Narrator cannot choose among these alternatives is the source of his anxiety; that he need not choose is the lesson he learns. With the aid of fideistic transcendence Chaucer learns, along with his Narrator, to make a virtue of necessity.

The literary virtues of that necessity are evident in the works that follow the *House of Fame*: the *Parliament of Fowls* (1382), *Troilus and Criseyde* (1385), the *Legend of Good Women* (1386), certain of the lyrics, and the *Canterbury Tales* as a unified work (1387–1400). The theme of conflicting alternatives remains, of course, a prominent one in Chaucer's work, though it is never again stated as nakedly as in the *House of Fame*, nor, after the lessons of the *House of Fame*, can it be treated in the same way.

The Narrator of the *Parliament of Fowls* is virtually im-mobilized with ambivalence when, in his dream, he is escorted by Scipio Africanus to a double gateway through which he must pass. On one side of the gate is inscribed a promise of pleasure, on the other a Dantesque warning of misery: it is an emblem of love itself, and the Narrator can-not choose:

> That oon me hette, that other dide me colde:
> No wit hadde I, for errour, for to chese,
> To entre or fleen, or me to save or lese.
>
> *(145–47)*

Once shoved in by his guide, the Narrator continues to encounter ambivalence. The attendants of Cupid include Pleasance and Curteysie, but also Wille and Craft "that kan and hath the myght/ To don by force a wyght to don folye" (220–21); Beauty and Youth, but also Flatery, Messagerie, and Meede. The fresh, vigorous fertility of Nature's Park is a foil for the stifling, dim atmosphere and calculated artifice of Venus's Temple. The plot of the poem, too, cen-ters around choice: the annual selection of mate granted the birds each Valentine's Day under Nature's supervision. But the natural process of selection is impeded by other and conflicting choices: several male eagles have chosen the female formel, and the formel herself has decided not to mate. In the ensuing debate different attitudes toward love are put forth by different birds, each commenting im-plicitly or directly on the others. The debate is not resolved, and the formel's choice is deferred; the lower orders of birds are allowed to mate, while the aristocratic birds are granted a year's delay. The moment of judgment is thus gracefully placed outside the poem.

In the sustained dialectic of the *Parliament* we can recog-nize some resemblance to the method of the *House of Fame*. Alternate possibilities about love are suggested in varying ways: symbolic landscape and architecture, abstract per-sonifications, prosopopoeia, and direct instruction such as Scipio's. No final commitment is made by the Narrator among these alternatives. Yet despite the lack of actual choice, one feels the *Parliament of Fowls* to be a satisfying work but the *House of Fame* not.

There are two main factors in this response. One is that the subject of the poem is no longer poetry itself, as it was in the *House of Fame*. The *Parliament* can therefore demonstrate the ambivalence of its subject (love) without calling itself into question. The other factor is the Narrator's role. Interestingly, the Narrator never once, after entering the Park, expresses anxiety over the possibilities available to him or to all of us. Nor does he express any judgment about the issues raised in the poem. Unlike Geffrey, he does not seem to consider choice either necessary or important. This amiable disinterestedness is due, I would suggest, to Chaucer's fideistic resolution of the problem of truth in art. No longer required to act as an instrument of choice, the Narrator is free to observe, to appreciate, and to record. Complexity, even ambivalence, is not for him the challenge it was for Geffrey; it produces no fear or uncertainty but is duly registered as the definition of love and of life, here in Nature's Park.

Such freedom is even more evident in *Troilus and Criseyde*, where the narrative voice itself becomes a source of ambivalence. The poem is a subtle and sophisticated exploration of will, of intention and action, of choice, motive, and result. The word "entente" and its variations appear again and again in the poem, forcing us finally to wonder, for each of the main characters, what was, after all, his will. No matter what Troilus, Criseyde, and Pandarus actually do, for good or ill, they constantly profess their good intentions. Troilus emerges as a person incapable of acting on his desires. His passivity, absurd at first, becomes finally repulsive; it suggests that in some sense he has not fully chosen what he desires, that he is, in his own way, as much as Criseyde, "of slydinge corage." Criseyde is quite capable of taking the initiative in bed—indeed she is forced by Troilus's passivity to do so at first—but in other circumstances she allows herself to be chosen (by her father, by

Troilus, by Diomede) or she lets others (Calchas, Pandarus) choose for her. Her own insufficiency of will, the inadequacy of her commitment, is shown in her repeated failures to assert herself: she does not refuse to leave Troy, she does not elope with Troilus, she does not resist Diomede. Of the three, only Pandarus has no trouble choosing and acting on his choice—except that his decisions are always for other people and in no way benefit himself. The three are tangled in a net of their own and others' conflicting desires and obligations; none has the strength to achieve his own salvation in a heroic choice or effort of will. Indeed the ending of the poem tells us that no such salvation is possible.

Choice is difficult not only for the main characters in *Troilus;* it is difficult for the Narrator also, and therefore it is difficult for the reader. We are constantly confronted with ambivalence: in puns; in the mixture of love-tragedy and bedroom farce; in the Narrator's deliberately confusing reportage and comment; in dramatic speeches which range from high-flown theological speculation to statements of shocking crudity, dishonesty, and bad taste. Only at the end of the poem, with Troilus's ascent to the eighth sphere, is ambivalence resolved. What was in the *Parliament of Fowls* the marvellous life-giving variety of Nature has become in *Troilus* the unreliable and emotionally draining nature of all that is not God. As I have noted earlier, the ending of the poem is the very model of fideism. Unreliability is as much the subject of *Troilus* as it is of the *House of Fame:* there the unreliability of literary tradition, here of experience itself. In a sense, then, *Troilus* takes up where the *House of Fame* leaves off: in the whirling, twig-built, labyrinthine House of Rumor, where truth and falsehood go about together so that no man can tell them apart, and where there is no man of authority great enough to separate them again.

In some of the *Canterbury Tales* choice is the theme. The *Wife of Bath's Tale* conforms in its structure to a fideistic pattern: choice is impossible in rational terms (shall the bride be fair and faithless, or ugly and chaste?); choice is evaded (the knight lets his supernatural bride decide) with happy result (she will be fair and faithful). The *Knight's Tale* shows the fragility of human choices and the weight of circumstance; the *Parson's Tale* exhorts the pilgrims and us to specific choices in matters of behavior:

> Stondeth upon the weyes, and seeth and axeth of olde pathes (that is to seyn, of olde sentences) which is the goode wey,/ and walketh in that wey, and ye shal fynde refresshynge for youre soules, etc./ Manye been the weyes espirituels that leden folk to oure Lord Jhesu Crist, and to the regne of glorie./ Of whiche weyes, ther is a ful noble wey and a ful convenable, which may nat fayle to man ne to womman that thurgh synne hath mysgoon fro the righte wey of Jerusalem celestial;/ and this wey is cleped Penitence. . . .
>
> (1. 75–80)

Other tales explore the consequences of a right or a wrong choice: the *Merchant's Tale*, the *Franklin's Tale*, the *Clerk's Tale*, and the *Man of Law's Tale*. As a group, though, all of the tales are exemplary in that they represent possible attitudes toward love, money, God, virtue, and one another: they show many possible choices without explicitly prescribing any. Even the *Parson's Tale* takes its place, if we want it to do so, as simply another possibility. Or, if we so choose, the *Parson's Tale* can represent ultimate truth. It seems after all to have done so for Chaucer, who ends his book with a prayer to

> Lord Jhesu Crist and his blisful Mooder, and alle the seintes of hevene,/ bisekynge hem that they from hennes forth unto my lyves ende sende me grace to biwayle my giltes, and to studie to the salvacioun of my soule, . . . thurgh the benigne grace of hym that is kyng of kynges and preest over alle

preestes, that boghte us with the precious blood of
his herte;/ so that I may been oon of hem at the
day of doom that shulle be saved.

(Parson's Tale, 1088–92)

It is a progression we have noticed before, from variety to
uniformity, from flawed human nature to divine perfection, from choices to prayer.

There is no truth to be had in the world; we hear that
message again in Chaucer's lyric "Truth," or "Balade de
Bon Conseil," (1386–90), probably the best known of his
shorter poems. "Flee fro the prees, and dwelle with soth-
fastnesse," the poem begins; and in its four stanzas the concept of truth is gradually developed from a general stoic
renunciation of involvement ("Tempest thee noght al
croked to redresse") into an explicitly Christian eschato-
logical vision:

> Crye him mercy, that of his hy goodnesse
> Made thee of noght, and in especial
> Draw unto him, and pray in general
> For thee, and eek for other, hevenlich mede,
> And trouthe thee shal delivere, it is no drede.

Nothing in this world merits our commitment or trust
("Her is non hoom, her nis but wildernesse"), so that it is
only Christ, truth incarnate, who can offer certainty.

The advantages of literary fideism are evident, I think,
in Chaucer's successful major works, for which the *House
of Fame* opened the way. The disadvantages are equally
obvious. Fideism differs from faith; it is a last resort, the
only kind of faith available to those who can find no reason
to believe. Chaucer is no ideological poet like Jean de
Meun or Dante. Religion is not his first idea but his last, so
that it enters the structure of his work not as a credible
solution to dialectic, but in fact as another term in dialectic.
Troilus's *contemptus mundi* fails to diminish our response
to the love story so vividly portrayed up to that point, and
the *Parson's Tale* fails to make us condemn the Wife of

Bath, who cheerfully incorporates many of the vices listed by the Parson. Chaucer fails, then, as a Christian poet: his success is with his art rather than with his ideology. That Chaucer is aware of some such distinction in his work, and that it makes him uneasy, is clear in the retraction appended to the *Canterbury Tales*. For all his "enditynges of worldly vanitees" the poet begs God's mercy and forgiveness. These writings, he says, include the love lyrics, all four dream-visions, a lost "Book of the Lion," and of the *Canterbury Tales* "thilke that sownen into synne"—most, in short, of his best known, liveliest, and most accomplished poetry. The works for which, on the contrary, he thanks Christ and Mary are the translation of Boethius and those of the *Tales* that are drawn from "bookes of legendes of seintes, and omelies, and moralitee, and devocioun." In practice, then, there is a certain "separation of truths" in Chaucer's art, but it is not a separation in which he finally believes. Ultimately the fideistic poet succeeds in spite of himself, for his own best works are part of the phenomenal world he mistrusts, part of its relative truth, part of its mixed tradition and multivalent fame.

More than once in this study I have referred to Matthew Arnold. I have mentioned Arnold less because he was a penetrating critic of Chaucer than because his experience as poet and scholar seems to me in important ways to resemble Chaucer's, especially that aspect of Chaucer's experience which is described in the *House of Fame*. Pluralism—less neutrally, indecisiveness—is characteristic of both writers. Both of them value the past but cannot derive from it sustenance adequate to the demands of the present. Both are profoundly concerned with conflict, whether social, moral, intellectual or physical, and with the necessity to weigh, balance, and choose.

That Chaucer and Matthew Arnold lived in periods of especially intense social conflict and rapid change is not, I think, irrelevant to the literary similarities I have noted. Henri Pirenne wrote that "the whole of the fourteenth century, like the whole of the nineteenth, was shaken by

the struggles of democracy."[1] More precisely, both centuries
were shaken by class struggle. In Chaucer's time the lay
and ecclesiastical feudal oligarchy had begun to be challenged by a newly rich bourgeoisie: importers and export-
ers, wool merchants, burgesses, owners of business. This
class had begun to assert for itself in Parliament and at
court, in towns and port cities, a social and political role
commensurate with its wealth.[2] But what was new in the
fourteenth century was old in the nineteenth, for by Arnold's time that same bourgeoisie had become itself the
ruling class. It was being challenged in turn by the prole-
tariat in Chartist rallies, in the trade union movement, the
abortive revolutions of 1848, the Paris Commune of 1871,
and the international communist movement, to which
Arnold's fellow poet William Morris lent his support.

Neither Chaucer nor Matthew Arnold allied himself
firmly with the old or with the new order. On balance
Chaucer seems to prefer entrepreneurial vitality—like that

1. Henri Pirenne, *A History of Europe* (New York, 1958), 2: 103.
2. Class struggle is a particularly complex phenomenon during the
Middle Ages. The bourgeoisie as a whole was continually engaged in
an effort to extort concessions from the governing aristocratic clique.
It did so sometimes by violent demonstrations, as with the revolt of
the burgesses of Bristol (1312) or the London riots of 1377 against John
of Gaunt, and sometimes by parliamentary maneuver, as in the "good
parliament" of 1376. However, the bourgeoisie itself was divided into
more and less prosperous sections which attempted to dominate one
another: a conflict evident, for example, in the London riots of 1383
over Nicholas Brembre's election to the mayoralty as representative of
the wealthy and powerful grocer's guild. The bourgeoisie as a whole
was challenged in turn by its employees—urban artisans and workers—
in continual strikes and revolts in England and on the continent. And
a united front of English artisans, peasants, and agricultural laborers
against the bourgeoisie and the feudal regime culminated in the rebel-
lion of 1381.
I have focused on the struggle of the bourgeoisie for two reasons.
First, it is Chaucer's own class: his father was a wine merchant and
Chaucer himself a civil servant. Second, it succeeded; that is, it won
state power and became the European ruling class. For both these
reasons it is more relevant to Chaucer's work than is the struggle of
other classes.

of the Wife of Bath, businesswoman and hedonist—to such hollow good form as the Prioress's. He shows us that such vitality may be opportunistic and self-indulgent, but that it is a life-force, a principle of movement, progressive as the class which the Wife of Bath on a modest scale represents. By Arnold's time, the sensitive intellectual could find little to praise in the bourgeoisie. In Thomas Carlyle's view, industrial capital had cast a spell on the land, condemning it to a living death of poverty-in-wealth. Arnold, too, despised the philistine bourgeoisie, but he saw no serious social alternative. The possibility of a new order did not exist for him as it did for his contemporaries Karl Marx, Friedrich Engels, and William Morris. Acknowledging no new source of cultural vitality, Arnold could create only images of failure, isolation, and despair, images of a world which has

> neither joy, nor love, nor light,
> Nor certitude, nor peace, nor help for pain. . . .

Contemporary poets have not resolved the dilemma of bourgeois culture any more satisfactorily than Matthew Arnold did, though the alternatives are much more obvious today than they were in Arnold's time. The late Charles Olson described—indeed exemplified—the condition of the poet who, perceiving the decadence of bourgeois culture, can neither reject it nor ally himself with revolutionary socialism:

> I thought of the E on the stone, and of what Mao said
> la lumiere"
>   but the kingfisher
> de l'aurore"
>   but the kingfisher flew west
> est devant nous!
>   he got the color of his breast
>   from the heat of the setting sun! . . .
> It nests at the end of a tunnel bored by itself in a

bank. There, six or eight white and translucent eggs
are laid, on fishbones not on bare clay, on bones
thrown up in pellets by the birds.
                    On these rejectamenta
(as they accumulate they form a cup-shaped structure)
    the young are born.
And, as they are fed and grow, this nest of excrement
    and decayed fish becomes
                    a dripping, fetid mass
Mao concluded:
            nous devons
                nous lever
                    et agir! . . .
    I pose you your question:
shall you uncover honey / where maggots are?
    I hunt among stones
                    (*"The Kingfishers"* [*1949*])

Chaucer's pluralism, his inability (or refusal) to commit
himself wholeheartedly to the past or to the present, his
ironic treatment of intellectual systems: these attitudes
are with us still. They help us to recognize in Chaucer's
poetry early versions of our own dilemma, just as we recog-
nize in the social events of Chaucer's time the roots of our
own historical experience. Insofar as that pluralism causes
us to recoil from the historical future, it is our "fantome
and illusion," and no fideistic leap of faith will help us to
transcend the choices confronting us. But if the *House of
Fame* can clarify anything for us it is the potential sterility
of being unable to choose.

Index

Index

Dante (cont.)
ideology of, 118; natural
place in, 72; on Orpheus, 90
Dares Phrygius, 94, 98–99
David, 95
Day, M., 39n
De Aeternitate Mundi (Siger
de Brabant), 16
De Arte Honesti Amandi,
31–32
De Caelo et Mundo, 20, 72
Decameron, 29
De Consolatione Philosophiae,
83–84, 89, 91, 110
Dedalus, 79–80, 104
De Excidio Troiae Historia, 98
Deidamia, 97
De Monarchia, 66
Denifle, H., 13n
Denomy, Alexander, 21n
De Raptu Proserpinae, 102
De Republica, 80
Desert, as setting, 58, 60, 69
Dialectics: confrontation with
Christian doctrine, 8–21;
danger of, 8–14; of Eagle's
monologue, 75–76, 79; re-
ligion as term in, 118;
structural, 76. *See also* Logic
Dictys Cretensis, 94, 98–99
Dido: character of, 51–54;
Chaucer's attitude toward,
53n; complaint of, 52-53, 54,
56; seduction of, 50, 51-53;
sources on, 25, 48, 49–56;
story of, 25, 46–47, 50–55,
104. *See also* Aeneas
Differentiarum, 62
Diomede, 116
Divine Comedy, 69, 72
Dobb, Maurice, 5n
Doctrine, Christian, 103;
confrontation with dialectics,
8–21; and transcendence of
choice, 31–32, 83. *See also*
Faith

Donaldson, E. Talbot, 2, 25–26,
53n
Double truth. *See* Separation
of truths
Doubt: transcendence of, 84;
value of, 11
Douglas, Gavin, 25
Dreams: as creativity, 44, 45–
46; as inspiration, 113; relation to composition, 44–
46; skepticism about, 44, 45,
46; validity of, 37–43. *See
also* Dream-vision
Dream-vision: advantages of,
37–38; authentication of, 38–
43; date of, 43; locus of, 58;
terminology of, 59-60;
validity of, 44, 46
Dual reputation, 48–56, 90–91,
92–93, 99, 100–101, 113
Duhem, Pierre, 74n
Eagle, 60, 104; character of,
74; description of Fame's
palace, 70–71; lack of logic,
74–76, 79; literary tradition
of, 69, 74; monologue, 3,
70-71, 74-75, 79; moralizing
of, 82–83; on natural place,
71, 73, 75; optimism of, 83;
pomposity of, 54, 74; trip to
House of Rumor, 105
Einhard, 42n
Empiricus, Sextus, 7n
Ending, lack of, 3, 108–9
Engels, Friedrich, 21 ,109, 121
Envious-detractors topos, 42n–
43n
Ephemeris Belli Troiani, 98
Epic: conventions, rejection of,
98, 101; fiction as, 34; use of,
54–55
Erigena, John Scotus, 8–9
Eternity: fear of, 78, 79;
question of, 15–16
Eucharist, 9, 18
Eurydice, 90